# speakout 2ND EDITION

## Starter
## Workbook

T0385813

Frances Eales • Steve Oakes
Stephanie Dimond-Bayir

# CONTENTS

# CONTENTS

## NUMBERS 1–10

**1** A Write the numbers in the puzzle.

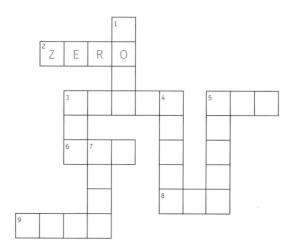

| Across | Down |
|--------|------|
| **2)** 0 | **1)** 4 |
| **3)** 3 | **3)** 2 |
| **5)** 6 | **4)** 8 |
| **6)** 1 | **5)** 7 |
| **8)** 10 | **7)** 9 |
| **9)** 5 | |

B ▶ L.1 Listen and write the next number.

*You hear:* 1, 2 …
*You write:* 3

1 ___*3*___      4 _____

2 _____      5 _____

3 _____      6 _____

## INTERNATIONAL ENGLISH

**2** A Circle six words.

B What's the word stress? Complete the table with the words from Exercise 1A.

| O | Oo | oO |
|---|----|----|
|   |    | ho<u>tel</u> |
|   |    |    |
|   |    |    |
|   |    |    |

C ▶ L.2 Listen and check. Then listen and repeat.

## CLASSROOM LANGUAGE

**3** A Put the words in the correct order to make sentences.

1 understand. / don't / I
  *I don't understand.*
2 Sorry, / page? / which
  _____
3 you / Can / please? / that, / repeat
  _____
4 English? / *autobus* / in / What's
  _____
5 it, / say / you / Can / please?
  _____
6 don't / I / Sorry, / know.
  _____

B Complete the conversations with the sentences from Exercise 3A.

1 **A:** We don't use verbs that way in our language.
  **B:** *I don't understand.*
2 **A:** _____
  **B:** It's *bus.*
3 **A:** _____
  **B:** Seven.
4 **A:** I'm Marek.
  **B:** _____
  **A:** Marek.
5 **A:** What's *casa* in English?
  **B:** _____
6 **A:** U-n-d-e-r-s-t-a-n-d.
  **B:** _____
  **A:** OK. Understand.

C ▶ L.3 Listen and check.

**4** Add vowels (*a, e, i, o, u*) to complete the useful phrases.

1 G o o d   m o rn i ng
2 G_ _ d n_ ght
3 H_ ll_
4 G_ _d _v_n_ng
5 G_ _d _ft_rn_ _n
6 H_

## GRAMMAR

### BE: I/YOU

**1** Write the negative sentences (–) or questions (?).

1 I'm from Spain. (–)   _I'm not from Spain._
2 You're a teacher. (?)   _Are you a teacher?_
3 I'm Sue Green. (–)   _____
4 You're in the
   Hilton Hotel. (–)   _____
5 I'm in room 2. (?)   _____
6 You're from
   Canada. (?)   _____
7 You're a student. (–)   _____
8 I'm late. (?)   _____

**2** Complete the conversations using the prompts.

1 A: Hi, / where / you?
   _Hi, where are you?_
   B: I / on the bus.
   _____
   _____

2 A: you / from England?
   _____
   B: No, I / not. I / from
   Scotland.
   _____
   _____

3 A: Hi. I / John Smith.
   _____
   B: I / John Smith, too. Nice /
   meet you.
   _____
   _____

4 A: you / from / Australia?
   _____
   _____
   B: Yes, / am. / I / from /
   Sydney.
   _____
   _____

## VOCABULARY

### COUNTRIES

**3 A** Add the vowels to make countries

1 (add **a** or **e**)
   _E_ ngl _a_ nd
   Ir _ l _ nd
   G _ rm _ ny

2 (add **a** or **u**)
   R _ ssi _
   _ _ str _ li _
   T _ rkey

3 (add **a** or **o**)
   J _ p _ n
   P _ l _ nd
   S _ uth _ fric _

4 (add **a** or **i**)
   Ch _ n _
   Br _ z _ l
   Sp _ _ n
   _ t _ ly

**B** What's the word stress? Complete the table with the countries in Exercise 3A.

| [1]O |
|---|
| |
| |

| [2]Oo |
|---|
| England |
| |

| [3]oO |
|---|
| |
| |

| [4]Ooo |
|---|
| |
| |

| [5]oOoo |
|---|
| |
| |

**C** ▶ 1.1 Listen and check. Then listen again and repeat.

## READING

4 A Read OpenChat and complete the information.

| Who? | deni89 | claudio327 | vera99 |
|---|---|---|---|
| Where now? | 1 *Mexico* | 3 | 5 |
| Where from? | 2 | 4 | 6 |

B Write the name(s) of the speakers.
1 'Good evening.'          *Claudio, ...*
2 'Good afternoon!'    _____
3 'Good coffee.'         _____
4 'Are you in Europe?    _____
5 'Bad pizza.'          _____
6 'Hello!'             _____

## WRITING

### CAPITAL LETTERS

5 Correct ten mistakes with capital letters in the sentences.

           *W*
1 I'm w/ei Ling and i'm from beijing in China.

2 I'm eva. I'm a Teacher from Germany.

3 I'm maria, from Rome, and i'm a student of english.

4 Good Morning. I'm Ahmet, from turkey.

## OpenChat.com

| **deni89** | **claudio327** | **vera99** |
|---|---|---|
| Good morning! | | |
| | Good evening! | |
| Good evening? Are you in Europe? | | |
| | No, I'm in Australia. | |
| Are you in Sydney? | | |
| | No, I'm not. I'm in Perth. | |
| Are you from Australia? | | |
| | No, I'm from Italy. I'm a tourist in Australia. Where are you from? | |
| I'm from Venezuela. But I'm in Mexico now. | | |
| | | Hello! Hello! |
| | Hello! Where are you? | |
| | | I'm in Johannesburg, South Africa. |
| Are you from South Africa? | | |
| | | No, from Portugal. |
| But you're in South Africa . . . so good afternoon! | | |
| | | Yeah. Good morning and good evening! |
| | | Yes, I am. And you? |
| Are you in an internet café? | | |
| I'm in a pizza restaurant. | | |
| | Me too. I'm in a pizza restaurant! | |
| | | Good pizza? |
| | No. Bad pizza. Good coffee. And you? | |
| | | Good coffee. No pizza. |

# VOCABULARY

## JOBS

**1 A** Find eight jobs in the puzzle.

| | | | | | | | | | | |
|---|---|---|---|---|---|---|---|---|---|---|
| S | D | O | C | T | O | R | B | F | P | O |
| I | C | B | U | E | O | M | U | Q | S | L |
| N | H | O | V | J | D | N | S | Z | F | D |
| G | T | A | X | I | D | R | I | V | E | R |
| E | E | B | B | O | J | M | N | W | W | U |
| R | A | H | T | I | U | D | E | A | W | D |
| I | C | Q | Y | D | E | T | S | I | K | A |
| O | H | Q | U | M | R | L | S | T | X | S |
| H | E | A | C | T | O | R | M | E | P | V |
| X | R | G | R | R | E | K | A | R | Y | C |
| Z | R | J | E | N | G | I | N | E | E | R |

**B** Write the jobs in the correct place under the pictures.

1 _____

2 _____

3 _____

4 _____

5 _____

6 _____

7 _____

8 _____

**2 A** Write *a* or *an* in the correct place in the sentences.

*an*
1 I'm⁄ American student.

2 You're New York taxi driver.

3 Are you actor?

4 I'm engineer from Madrid.

5 I'm hotel waiter.

6 Are you singer?

**B** ▶ 1.2 Listen and check. Then listen and repeat.

# LISTENING

**3 A** ▶ 1.3 Listen to the conversations. Where is each conversation? Circle the correct options.
1 **a)** classroom
  **b)** business conference
2 **a)** hotel
  **b)** hospital

**B** Listen again and complete the information.

| | Job | Country |
|---|---|---|
| **Ed** | *student* | |
| **Cathy** | | |
| **Misaki** | | |
| **Anna** | | |
| **Lynn Baker** | | |
| **Jan** | | |

**C** Listen again and underline the correct alternatives.
1 Am I in the *Japanese/English* class?
2 *No problem/thank you.* I'm Ed.
3 And you, are you *Spanish/English*?
4 It's my first *time/day* here.
5 Look, here's a *doctor/nurse*.
6 Are you from *Russia/Poland*, too?

# GRAMMAR

## BE: HE/SHE/IT

**4 A** Look at the pictures and complete the information.

1 _____*He's*_____ in China.
2 _____*She's*_____ from Lima.
3 _____ in the USA.
4 _____ in France.

**B** Put the words in the correct order to make questions.

1 he / Where / is / China? / in
   *Where is he in China?*
2 is / Lima? / Where
   _____
3 it / Los Angeles / Is / in / Washington? / or
   _____
4 France? / she / is / Where / in
   _____

**C** Look at the photos and circle the correct answers to questions 1–4 in Exercise 4B.

1 a) The Summer Palace    b) The Great Wall
2 a) in Peru              b) in Colombia
3 a) Los Angeles          b) Washington
4 a) Paris                b) Las Vegas

**5 A** Complete the conversations with the verb *be*.

**Conversation 1**
A: Good morning. I'¹___*m*___ Sylvia White.
B: Ah, yes. Mrs White. You' ²_____ in Room 9.
A: ³_____ Mr Martin here?
B: Yes, he ⁴_____. He' ⁵_____ in Room 8.

**Conversation 2**
A: Hi, Pat. Nice camera!
B: Thanks.
A: ⁶_____ it a Panasonic?
B: No, it ⁷_____. It's an Olympus.

**Conversation 3**
A: Hi, Helena!
B: Oh, hello, Marcus. Marcus, this ⁸_____ Jackie, from Australia.
A: Hi, Jackie. Nice to meet you. ⁹_____ you here on holiday?
C: No, I' ¹⁰_____ here on business.

**B** ▷ 1.4 Listen and check.

## VOCABULARY

### THE ALPHABET

**1 A** Underline the letter with a different sound.

1 S <u>R</u> N F
2 A K J E
3 G B I T
4 H U W Q
5 V C Y P
6 X Z L D

**B** ▷ 1.5 Listen and check. Then listen and repeat.

**2** ▷ 1.6 Listen and complete the names.

| Class register | | |
|---|---|---|
| | **First Name** | **Surname** |
| 1 | Alexandra | *Baecher* |
| 2 | _____ | Mancini |
| 3 | Louise | _____ |
| 4 | _____ | Watson |
| 5 | Meilin | _____ |
| 6 | _____ | Kean |

## FUNCTION

### GIVING PERSONAL INFORMATION

**3** Write the questions in the conversation.

A: [1]*What's your surname* ?
B: It's Thompson.
A: [2] _____ ?
B: T-h-o-m-p-s-o-n.
A: Thank you. [3] _____ ?
B: Jack.
A: And [4] _____ ?
B: I'm Irish.
A: [5] _____, Mr Thompson?
B: I'm a police officer.
A: Oh! [6] _____, sir?
B: 0782 1129 1827.
A: Thank you, sir. One last question, sir.
[7] _____ ?
B: jthompson823@mail.net.
A: Thank you very much.

## LEARN TO

### CHECK SPELLING

**4** ▷ 1.7 Listen to the information and correct the email addresses. There may be more than one mistake in each address.

1 y
evesbedi373@yippee.com

2 yohana999@gomail.com

3 heideho251@itmail.com

4 gorgelopez@toggle.com

## VOCABULARY

### NOUNS

**5 A** Put the letters in the correct order to make nouns.

1 amne      *name*
2 breunm      _____
3 neohp      _____
4 meial      _____
5 alytniianot      _____
6 dsreads      _____
7 mersuna      _____

**B** Add vowels (*a, e, i, o, u*) to complete the sentences.

1 Wh_a_t's y_o_ _u_r n_a_m_e_?
2 H_ll_.
3 _'m fr_m Sp__n.
4 G__d _v_n_ng.
5 Th_nk y__.
6 Wh_t's y__r ph_n_ n_mb_r?
7 My s_rn_m_'s Ly.
8 Anabella __s _ st_d_nt.

# 2 PEOPLE

## VOCABULARY

### FAMILY

ROB
MEG
ALAN
KATY

**1 A** Write the family words to complete the puzzle. In the grey boxes find the answer to the question: *What's in the photo?*

```
                    1 d  a  u  g  h  t  e  r
      2 b  r  
                  3 f     t
                4       a  r  e        5 s
                        p              
                        y              n
              6    w  i
      7 h  u
                  8       o  t  h
                9    s     s  t
      10 c  h
                        y
```

**B** Look at the photo and the crossword. Write the family words.

Alan:           *father*        *husband*
Meg:            _____      _____
Alan and Meg:   _____
Rob:            _____      _____
Katy:           _____      _____
Rob and Katy:   _____

## GRAMMAR

### BE: YOU/WE/THEY

**2 A** Complete the sentences with *you, we* or *they*.

1 Magda and Wislaw are Polish, but ___they___ 're in England now.
2 You and Sven are married, but _____ aren't happy.
3 Yvette and I are friends, and _____ 're both twenty-one today.
4 My friends are very nice, but _____ 're all on holiday.
5 Chen and I are waiters in a restaurant, and _____ 're good friends, too.
6 His two brothers are in my class, and _____ 're good students.
7 You and Toni are brother and sister, and _____ 're both chefs!
8 My family is big, and _____ 're very close.

**B** Write the conversations using the prompts.

1 **A:** you / students?
   *Are you students?*
   **B:** No, / we /. We / teachers.
   *No, we aren't. We're teachers.*
2 **A:** they / from France?
   _____
   **B:** Yes, / they /. They / from Paris.
   _____
3 **A:** you and Charlie / brothers?
   _____
   **B:** No, / we /. We / friends.
   _____
4 **A:** you / pilot?
   _____
   **B:** No, / I /. I / actor.
   _____
5 **A:** Jack and Diane / English?
   _____
   **B:** No, / they /. They / American.
   _____
6 **A:** your car / new?
   _____
   **B:** No, / it /. It / old.
   _____

## READING

**3 A** Read texts 1–3 and match them with pictures A–C.

**A**

1  _James_  2 _____  3 _____

**B**

4 _____   5 _____

**C**

6 _____   7 _____

**1**

_This is my mother and father, and my sister Jenny.
And me, of course. We're at home in the garden.
My other sister, Cindy, isn't in the photo – it's her camera!
Jenny's a good sister, and a good friend.
Cindy is nice, but she's never at home._  **(Ricky)**

**2**

_This is my grandfather, my grandmother, my brother
Dan and me. We're in my flat in Newcastle. My
grandfather's 86 in this photo. It's his birthday._

(Miranda)

**3**

_This is me and my husband James. We're on holiday in
Spain, on the beach. It's a good place for a holiday – it's
very beautiful. This is our son, Tom. He's 12 years old._

(Sam)

**B** Read the texts again and write the names on the pictures.

**C** Write the names. Who says:

1  'It's a nice cake, Miranda! Thank you.'  _Granddad_
2  **A:** 'It's a beautiful beach! What do you think?'
   _____
   **B:** 'I love it, Mum.' _____
3  'Hey, Mum. Where are Cindy and Ricky?'
   _____
4  'Happy Birthday, Granddad!' _____
5  **A:** 'I'm hot, Dad. Is the sea cold?' _____
   **B:** 'No, it isn't. It's nice.' _____
6  'I'm not in the photo. It's my camera!' _____

_Mum = mother   Dad = father   Granddad = grandfather_

## WRITING

### CONTRACTIONS

**4 A** Read the messages and number them in the correct order.

a) Hi, Paul. Lisa is not here. Her phone is here. I am Sarah, a friend. ☐

b) He is a student. We are in the same class. ☐

c) Oh hi, Sarah. Where is Lisa? ☐

d) Yes, he is. ☐

e) Is he from Japan? ☐

f) Who is Kenji? ☐

g) Hi, Lisa. It is Paul. Pizza? 1

h) She is with Kenji. They are at the cinema. ☐

**B** Rewrite the messages in the correct order using contractions.

1  _Hi, Lisa. It's Paul. Pizza?_
2  _____
3  _____
4  _____
5  _____
6  _____
7  _____
8  _____

## VOCABULARY

### NUMBERS 11–100

**1 A** Write the numbers.

1  64  *sixty-four*
2  _____ *13* _____ thirteen
3  12 _____
4  _____ fifty
5  100 _____

6  _____ eleven
7  45 _____
8  _____ thirty-one
9  76 _____
10 _____ twenty-six

**B** Complete the quiz with numbers from Exercise 1A. Use your dictionary to help you.

# NUMBERS, NUMBERS, NUMBERS

1  States in the United States of America _____ *50*

2  Letters in the alphabet _____

3  People in a football team _____

4  Countries in South America _____

5  Days in January, March and May _____

6  1 + 2 + 3 + 4 + 5 + 6 + 7 + 8 + 9 _____

7  ___ million people in the UK _____

8  Letters in *international* _____

9  The age of Albert Einstein (1879–1955) _____

10 Cents in one euro _____

## LISTENING

**2 A** Read the information about a radio programme. What jobs are in the information?

# All in the family

Today's programme is about people in families with the same job. We ask singers, actors, chefs and sportspeople, 'Your parents and family have the same job. Is it a problem?'

**B** ▷ 2.1 Listen to part of the radio programme and underline the correct alternatives.

1  a) His family are *actors/singers*.
   b) It *is/isn't* a problem.
2  a) Her family are *chefs/sportspeople*
   b) It *is/isn't* a problem.

**C** Listen again and complete the tables.

**1**

| Person | Job |
| --- | --- |
| Ben | *actor* |
| His father | |
| His mother | |
| His sister | |
| Jack | |
| Dave | |

**2**

| Person | Job |
| --- | --- |
| Celeste | |
| Her mother | |
| Her father | |
| Her sister | |

# GRAMMAR
## POSSESSIVE ADJECTIVES

**3** Underline the correct alternatives.

1 *Their/They're* on holiday in Spain and *their/they're* hotel is on the beach.
2 *I/My* job is in the city, but *I/my* house is in the countryside.
3 *Our/We're* teacher is great, and *our/we're* very good students.
4 The island? *Its/It's* small and *its/it's* beach is beautiful.
5 *My/I'm* a taxi driver and *my/I'm* car is a Mercedes.
6 *Her/She* father is American and *her/she* mother's Canadian.
7 *Our/We're* hotel is nice, but *our/we're* in the city on business.
8 *My/I* flat is small, but *my/I'm* alone.
9 *Its/It's* my book, and *its/it's* a good book.

**4 A** ▶ **2.2** Listen and circle the word you hear.

1 her / his
2 she / her
3 she / he
4 He's / His
5 he's / his
6 our / their
7 our / their

**B** Listen again and write the sentences. Then listen and repeat.

1 *What's her job?*
2 _____
3 _____
4 _____
5 _____
6 _____
7 _____

**5** Complete the sentences with the words in the box. You don't need to use two of the words.

your your his our my her its their

1 Is it _____your_____ phone?

2 That's _____ bus!

3 It isn't _____ dog.

4 Wow! Who is _____ hairdresser?

5 _____ taxi is here.

6 Are you _____ mother?

# VOCABULARY

## FEELINGS

**1** Look at the pictures and complete the crossword.

Down:

Across:

# FUNCTION

## MAKING SUGGESTIONS

**2 A** Complete the conversation.

**A:** Let's ¹h_ave_____ a break.

**B:** No, let's ²n_____ stop. ³L_____ work.

**A:** No, let's not ⁴w_____ now.

**B:** Why not? What's the ⁵pr_____?

**A:** ⁶I_____ tired!

**B:** Oh. Yes, I'm tired, ⁷t_____.

**A:** Let's ⁸st_____.

**B:** Good ⁹i_____!

**B** ▷ 2.3 Listen and check. Then listen and repeat.

# LEARN TO

## RESPOND TO SUGGESTIONS

**3 A** ▷ 2.4 Listen to the pairs of conversations. In which conversation, a) or b), does the person sound interested?

1 ____b____

2 _____

3 _____

4 _____

**B** ▷ 2.5 Listen again and repeat.

## VOCABULARY REVIEW

### 1 A Add the vowels to the words in each group.

**1**

(add **o** or **e**)

br_o_th_e_r

tw__nty-__n__

busin__ssw__man

b__r__d

**2**

(add **e** or **i**)

t__r__d

ch__ldr__n

__ng__n____r

s__v__nty-____ght

**3**

(add **a**, **o** or **u**)

f__rty-f____r

h__sb__nd

__ct__r

c__ld

**4**

(add **e**, **i** or **u**)

th__rsty

tax__ dr__v__r

th__rty-f__v__

da__ght__r

**B** In each group find: a job (J), a family word (F), a number (N) and an adjective (A).

brother   *F*

**C** What's the word stress? Find six words with the pattern Oo.

**O o**

*brother*

**D** ▶ R1.1 Listen and repeat.

## GRAMMAR BE

### 2 A Complete the text with the correct form of *be* in the positive (+) or negative (–).

# A family of pilots

Rafael Illanes [1] _____*is*_____ from Brazil. He's a pilot from a family of pilots. 'My family [2]_____ all over the world. My brother, Fabio, is a pilot with Aeroflot. He and his wife, Svetlana, [3]_____ in Moscow, but Svetlana [4]_____ Russian, she's Polish (and she isn't a pilot, she [5]_____ a doctor).

My sister, Emilia, is in Korea, and she and her husband, Pehuen, [6]_____ pilots, too. Their children, Luis and Antonia, [7]_____ fifteen and seventeen.

My parents [8]_____ from the city of Brasilia, but they [9]_____ in Brazil now, they're in Greece. Their summer house [10]_____ in a village in the countryside in Greece. It's an old house and very beautiful. My parents are seventy-three years old and they're retired – retired pilots!'

**B** Write the questions for Rafael.

1 Where / you / from?   *Where are you from?*
2 What / your / job?   _____
3 your / brother / married?   _____
4 Where / his / wife / from?   _____
5 Where / Emilia and Pehuen?   _____
6 How old / their children?   _____
7 your parents / in Brazil?   _____
8 their summer house / in the city?   _____

**C** Answer the questions in Exercise 2B.

1 *I'm from Brazil.* _____
2 _____
3 _____
4 _____
5 _____
6 _____
7 _____
8 _____

**GRAMMAR** POSSESSIVE ADJECTIVES

**3** Underline the correct alternatives.

**Conversation 1**

**A:** Excuse me, are they [1]you're/_your_ children?
**B:** Yes, they are.
**A:** [2]They're/Their beautiful girls.
**B:** [3]They/Their aren't girls! [4]They're/Their a boy and a girl.
**A:** Oh, sorry.
**B:** That's OK. [5]His/He's name's Mark and [6]she's/her's Jane.
**A:** Well, [7]they're/their beautiful children!

**Conversation 2**

**A:** Are [8]you/your a tourist?
**B:** No, I'm in Frankfurt on business.
**A:** Oh, is [9]your/our business in Frankfurt?
**B:** [10]My/Its business is in London. [11]My/Its name is 'Compu-market'.
**A:** Is it a big business?
**B:** No, [12]its/it's very small.

**VOCABULARY** THE ALPHABET

**4 A** ▶ R1.2 Listen and write the airport codes.

> # WORLD
> # AIRPORTS ✈
>
> | | | |
> |---|---|---|
> | 1  _WAW_ | 5 _____ | 9 _____ |
> | 2 _____ | 6 _____ | 10 _____ |
> | 3 _____ | 7 _____ | 11 _____ |
> | 4 _____ | 8 _____ | 12 _____ |

**B** Match the airport codes in Exercise 4A with the cities/countries in the box.

| Warsaw, Poland _WAW_ | Ottawa, Canada _____ | Seoul, Korea _____ |
|---|---|---|
| Berlin, Germany _____ | Kuala Lumpur, Malaysia _____ | Ankara, Turkey _____ |
| Washington, America _____ | Moscow, Russia _____ | Beijing, China _____ |
| Helsinki, Finland _____ | Rome, Italy _____ | Amman, Jordan _____ |

**C** ▶ R1.3 Listen and check.

**FUNCTION** MAKING SUGGESTIONS; GIVING PERSONAL INFORMATION

**5 A** Complete the sentences with the words in the box.

| ~~have~~  restaurant  go  Good  hours  'm  's  not |
|---|

a) Yeah, me too. Let's ___have___ a drink.   _____
b) OK, OK. Let's _____ to the café.   _____
c) Oh, no! Five _____ in the airport!   _1_
d) No, let's _____ go to the café. Let's go to the restaurant.   _____
e) _____ idea!   _____
f) Yeah, five hours. Hey, I _____ thirsty.   _2_
g) Let _____ go to the café.   _____
h) The _____ ? No, the café.   _____

**B** Number the sentences in Exercise 5A in the correct order to complete the conversation.

**C** ▶ R1.4 Listen and check.

**6 A** Look at the information and write three questions.

Adél Gonta
475-1672
adel237@smail.com

1 _What's your name?_ _____
2 _____
3 _____

**B** ▶ R1.5 Listen and check.

**C** Listen again and correct the information.

## CHECK

Circle the correct option to complete the sentences.

1  A:  Are you from Beijing?
   B:  Yes, _____.
   a)  we're
   b)  we are
   c)  we aren't

2  Henry's _____.
   a)  singer
   b)  a taxi
   c)  a singer

3  A:  I'm tired.
   B:  Oh, _____ stop.
   a)  let not
   b)  let's not
   c)  let not's

4  A:  Are you married?
   B:  Yes, Mark is my _____.
   a)  brother
   b)  father
   c)  husband

5  A:  Is she an actress?
   B:  No, _____.
   a)  isn't
   b)  she not
   c)  she isn't

6  What's _____ name?
   a)  it's
   b)  it
   c)  its

7  He's from _____.
   a)  the USA
   b)  USA
   c)  American

8  A:  Am I right?
   B:  Yes, _____.
   a)  you're
   b)  your
   c)  you are

9  He's a good _____.
   a)  wait
   b)  waiter
   c)  wayter

10  _____ sit down.
   a)  Let
   b)  Let we
   c)  Let's

11  A:  What's your nationality?
    B:  I'm _____.
    a)  a singer
    b)  Italy
    c)  Brazilian

12  I _____ Scott.
    a)  're
    b)  'm
    c)  be

13  _____ engineers.
    a)  They're
    b)  Their
    c)  There

14  A:  Are they your cats?
    B:  Yes. _____ names are Ralph and Wally.
    a)  Our
    b)  Their
    c)  Her

15  A:  I'm hungry.
    B:  Me too. Let's _____.
    a)  eat
    b)  read
    c)  have a drink

16  Jess _____ English.
    a)  is
    b)  she
    c)  aren't

17  Is Lynn your _____?
    a)  parents
    b)  children
    c)  daughter

18  What _____ surname?
    a)  's your
    b)  's
    c)  your

19  A:  How old are you?
    B:  I'm _____.
    a)  thirteen-seven
    b)  thirty-seven
    c)  thirty and seven

20  A:  Where are you from?
    B:  I'm from _____.
    a)  Russian
    b)  Russia
    c)  Rusha

RESULT    /20

## VOCABULARY

### THINGS

**1 A** Find eight objects.

tabletcomputerpenchairkeytableboxnotebookcup

**B** Write the plural of the words in Exercise 1A.

1  _tablet computers_      5  _____
2  _____        6  _____
3  _____        7  _____
4  _____        8  _____

**C** Write the plural of the words.

1  phone number    _phone numbers_
2  country          _____
3  classroom        _____
4  businessman      _____
5  bus              _____
6  student          _____
7  university       _____
8  child            _____
9  hotel manager    _____
10 glass            _____

## READING

**2 A** Check *invention* in your dictionary. Which inventions 1–8 are in the pictures?

1  paper        5  pizza
2  email        6  chocolate
3  pencil       7  wheelchair
4  aspirin      8  margarine

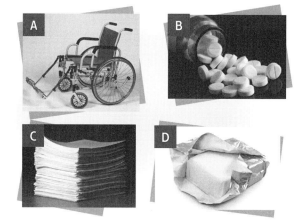

A   B
C   D

**B** Where are inventions 1–8 from? Match the country and the invention.

Italy   USA   Germany   France
Mexico   Spain   England   China

**C** Read the text and check your ideas.

# Where are they from?

Great inventions are international, but where are they from? Where is the wheelchair from? How about aspirin? And chocolate? Read and find out!

### Food

It's no surprise that pizza is from Italy, the invention of an Italian baker, Raffaele Esposito. Switzerland is famous for chocolate, but chocolate is in fact from Central America, from Mexico. And what about another food, margarine? Well, margarine is the invention of a Frenchman, Hippolyte Mège-Mouriès.

### Communications

The word 'paper' is from the Egyptian word 'papyrus', but paper is one of the great inventions of ancient China. And the pencil? That's from England. Now we don't communicate on paper very much, but by email. Email is the invention of an American, Ray Tomlinson. Tomlinson's first email was QWERTYUIOP!

### Health

Aspirin is from Germany, the invention of Felix Hoffman, for his ill father. And how about the wheelchair? The wheelchair is a Spanish invention. The first wheelchair was for King Philip II of Spain in 1554.

**D** Cover the text and write the invention for 1–5. Then read the text again and check your answers.

1  Raffaele Esposito        _pizza_
2  Felix Hoffman            _____
3  Hippolyte Mège-Mouriès   _____
4  King Philip II of Spain  _____
5  Ray Tomlinson            _____

# GRAMMAR
## THIS/THAT/THESE/THOSE

**3** Complete the conversations with *this*, *that*, *these* or *those*.

**1** ___*This*___ is my friend, Dave. Dave, _____ is Jim.

**2** Are _____ from Spain?

**3** Is _____ your car?

**4** _____ are my teeth!

**5** What's _____ in English?

**6** Are _____ your keys?

**4 A** Complete the sentences with the words in the box.

| ~~this~~ that these those is (x2) are (x2) |
| --- |

*this*
**1** Is ⋀ your book here on the table?
**2** What are boxes here on my chair?
**3** This my friend, Domingo.
**4** These my parents, Steve and Beth.
**5** Is a number 43 bus over there?
**6** Are your books over there?
**7** Who that woman with Harry?
**8** Who those children?

**B** Underline six examples of /s/ in the sentences in Exercise 4A.

*Is thi̱s your book?*

**C** Circle nine examples of /z/ in the sentences in Exercise 4A.

*Ⓘs this your book?*

**D** ▶ 3.1 Listen and check. Then listen and repeat.

**5 A** Make the sentences plural.
**1** This is my friend.
*These are my friends.*
_____

**2** That's her brother.
_____
_____

**3** Is that your chair?
_____
_____

**4** This is the new student.
_____
_____

**B** Make the sentences singular.
**1** Are those pictures old?
_____
_____

**2** These are my business cards.
_____
_____

**3** Who are these students?
_____
_____

**4** Those are Susan's keys.
_____
_____

## VOCABULARY

### COLOURS AND CLOTHES

**1** Find six words for colours and six words for clothes.

| T | S | W | E | A | T | E | R | H |
|---|---|---|---|---|---|---|---|---|
| R | B | R | O | W | N | S | S | A |
| O | J | T | G | E | H | A | T | B |
| U | F | K | S | Q | D | U | D | L |
| S | W | W | H | I | T | E | Z | U |
| E | J | B | I | P | Y | M | W | E |
| R | A | L | R | K | E | R | E | D |
| S | K | A | T | S | H | I | R | T |
| J | A | C | K | E | T | P | X | N |
| N | X | K | Y | E | L | L | O | W |

**2** Write the colour(s) of the things.

1 ___red___ , _____ and
_____
2 _____
3 _____
4 _____
5 _____
6 _____

## LISTENING

**3 A** Write the names of the clothes.

**B** ▶ 3.2 Listen to the conversations. Match the speakers with three of the pictures.

Speaker 1 _____
Speaker 2 _____
Speaker 3 _____

**C** Listen again. What is the speaker's favourite colour? Underline the correct alternatives.

Speaker 1    red / green / black
Speaker 2    blue / yellow / white
Speaker 3    brown / black / red

**D** What's your favourite colour? Why? Write two sentences.

_____
_____
_____

## GRAMMAR

### POSSESSIVE 'S

4 Add one 's to each conversation.

1 A: What is Lena_'s_ job?
   B: She's a teacher.
2 A: Where is Nasra coffee?
   B: It's over here.
3 A: Is Andy room number three *four* one or three *two* one?
   B: Let me check. It's three *four* one.
4 A: Who is that man over there?
   B: Oh, that's Paulo. He's my husband manager.
5 A: How old are Kamal brothers?
   B: Ali is thirteen and Omar is fourteen.
6 A: Who is Pilar?
   B: She's one of Maria friends from university.
7 A: Is this your bag, Andy?
   B: No, that's a woman bag!
8 A: What's your mother name?
   B: It's Olivia, Olivia Marr.
9 A: What's Lidia nationality?
   B: I think she's Argentinian.
10 A: Where's my coat?
   B: It's on Felipe chair.

5 Look at 's in the sentences. Is it possessive (P) or *is*?

1 Our cat's name is Ebony.          _P_
2 What's her surname?               _is_
3 Li's in Tokyo on business.        _____
4 Krystina's husband is Scottish.   _____
5 Sydney isn't Australia's capital city.  _____
6 Where's my phone?                 _____
7 My brother's a doctor in Uruguay. _____
8 A teacher's job is difficult.     _____

## WRITING

### LINKERS AND, BUT

6 Complete the replies with *and* or *but*.

1 That's a nice watch.
   a) Thanks. It's Swiss ____and____ it's very good.
   b) Thanks, _____ it isn't my watch. It's my daughter's watch.
   c) Thanks, it's nice, _____ it's not very good.

2 Are you cold?
   a) Yes, _____ I'm tired.
   b) No, _____ I'm tired.
   c) Yes, _____ I'm fine.

3 Is your coat black?
   a) Yes, _____ that isn't my coat.
   b) No, _____ my coat is in my car.
   c) Yes, _____ that's my coat, thanks.

4 Are those sunglasses new?
   a) Yes, _____ they're good.
   b) No, _____ they're good.
   c) No, _____ they're reading glasses, not sunglasses.

5 What's the homework?
   a) Two pages in the workbook. Pages 65 _____ 66.
   b) Pages 65 _____ 66 in the workbook.
   c) I think it's this page, _____ please check with Dimitri.

6 Hi, Chris. Is this your sister, Anne?
   a) Yes, _____ her name's not Anne. It's Anna with an 'a'.
   b) Yes, this is Anne _____ this is her friend, Carole.
   c) This is Anne, _____ she's my friend, not my sister.

## VOCABULARY
### FOOD AND DRINK

**1** Add vowels to make food and drink.

**Hot drinks**       **Cold drinks**
¹t _e_ _a_              ³c _ l _
²c _ ff _ _            ⁴m _ n _ r _ l  w _ t _ r

**Food**
⁵c _ k _
⁶s _ ndw _ ch

## FUNCTION
### ORDERING IN A CAFÉ

**2** ▷ 3.3 Listen and complete the orders.

**1**

Table 3

2 ___egg___ sandwiches, _____
bread, 1 espresso, 1_____.

**2**

Table 5

1 mineral water ( _____ )

_____ cakes.

**3**

Table 10

1_____, 1_____ mineral

water, 1 tea, 1_____.

**3** Put the words in the correct order to complete the conversation.

**A:** morning. / Good
   _Good morning._

**B:** we / two / mineral / Can / waters, / have / please?
   _____

**A:** sparkling? / Still / or
   _____

**B:** please. / still, / One / one / sparkling / and
   _____

**A:** else? / Anything
   _____

**B:** you. / thank / No,
   _____

**A:** that? / is / much / How
   _____

**B:** euros / That / five / fifty. / 's
   _____

## LEARN TO
### SAY PRICES

**4** Write the prices in dollars ($), euros (€) or pounds (£).

1  $15.30
   _fifteen dollars thirty_ _____

2  £19.50
   _____

3  €11.25
   _____

4  €8.10
   _____

5  $22.75
   _____

6  £1.99
   _____

## VOCABULARY
### OBJECTS

**5** Match 1–6 with a)–f).

| | | |
|---|---|---|
| 1 sparkling | **a)** bread |
| 2 egg | **b)** cake |
| 3 chocolate | **c)** euros |
| 4 white | **d)** sandwich |
| 5 espresso | **e)** coffee |
| 6 three | **f)** water |

**6** Match the pictures with four answers from Exercise 5.

# 4 LIFE

## VOCABULARY

### VERB PHRASES

**1 A** Add the correct letters to complete the verb phrases.

1 s t u d y Japanese
2 h _ _ _ a sister
3 w _ _ _ in an office
4 g _ to my room
5 d _ a grammar exercise
6 l _ _ _ with my family
7 l _ _ _ tea
8 d _ _ _ _ to work

**B** Cross out the incorrect alternative.

1 _____ to a café
  **a)** drive    **b)** go    **c)** ~~do~~
2 _____ a car
  **a)** drive    **b)** go    **c)** have
3 _____ English
  **a)** drive    **b)** study    **c)** like
4 _____ eight hours a day
  **a)** work    **b)** study    **c)** like
5 _____ homework
  **a)** do    **b)** have    **c)** live
6 _____ pizzas
  **a)** like    **b)** work    **c)** have
7 _____ at university
  **a)** go    **b)** study    **c)** work
8 _____ home
  **a)** study    **b)** go    **c)** drive

**C** Complete the sentences about you.

1 I like _____ .

2 I live _____ .

3 I have _____ .

4 I study/work _____ .

5 I go _____ .

6 I do _____ .

## READING

**2 A** Match forum entries 1–3 with photos A–C.

### Travel Forum: What's different?

**Where are you now? Send us a photo and tell us what's different about it for you.**

**1** What's different? It's very hot here and the shops in the old market are very different. The market is big and they have beautiful old jewellery and pottery. We're here on holiday and I like it very much – the people are great. The big problem for me is … well, it's very hot here, and I'm always thirsty.

**2** What's different? Not a lot. They have yellow taxis here. At home our taxis are black. The people are very friendly: they say 'Have a nice day!' all the time, the same as in films. That's different. I like the city a lot, but I'm surprised because it's very cold and I don't have my winter clothes.

**3** What's different? They have music, music everywhere: samba, lambada, bossa nova – it's great. The city is on the beach. That's different. We don't have beaches at home. The food's very good, too. I'm in my favourite café with an espresso and a hot 'pao de queijo' (cheese bread). The city is beautiful, but it has hundreds of tourists.

**B** Read the text again and complete the table.

| | What is different? | What is one problem? |
|---|---|---|
| 1 | **a)** *it's very hot*<br>**b)** | **c)** |
| 2 | **a)**<br>**b)** | **c)** |
| 3 | **a)**<br>**b)** | **c)** |

## GRAMMAR
### PRESENT SIMPLE: I/YOU/WE/THEY

**3** Look at the information in the table. Then complete the sentences about Brenda and her friends at university in Madrid.

| | Me (Brenda) | Maria and Laura |
|---|---|---|
| **1** speak Spanish | ✗ | ✓ |
| **2** read the newspaper | ✓ online | ✗ |
| **3** drive | ✓ | ✓ |
| **4** study | ✓ 4 hours/day | ✗ |
| **5** work | ✗ | ✓ restaurant in evenings |
| **6** listen to rock music | ✓ radio | ✓ smartphone |
| **7** like football | ✓ | ✓ |
| **8** have a boyfriend | ✗ | ✓ Raul and José |

1 Maria and Laura ___*speak*___ Spanish (they <u>are</u> Spanish), but they ___*speak*___ English with me. I <u>*don't speak*</u> Spanish.

2 I _____ the newspaper online. They _____ the newspaper – they aren't interested in the news.

3 We all _____, but we don't have a car.

4 I _____ for four hours in the evening. They aren't very good students and they _____!

5 In the evening they _____ at a restaurant – they're waitresses, but I _____.

6 We _____ to the same music. They _____ to music on their smartphones, but I _____ to the radio.

7 We _____ the same football team, Real Madrid.

8 They _____ boyfriends, Raul and José. I _____ a boyfriend.

**4** Write questions and short answers using the prompts.

1 A: you / have / brother?
   *Do you have a brother?*
   B: (+) <u>*Yes, I do.*</u>

2 A: I / write / my name here?
   _____?
   B: (+) _____.

3 A: we / work / in the evenings?
   _____?
   B: (–) _____.

4 A: your children / like / the countryside?
   _____?
   B: (–) _____.

5 A: your parents / live / in the city?
   _____?
   B: (+) _____.

6 A: you / study / Spanish?
   _____?
   B: (+) _____.

**5 A** Complete the questions.

A: What [1] *'s your name* ?
B: Philip, Philip Moore.
A: Where [2] _____?
B: I live in London and Prague.
A: Why [3] _____ in two cities?
B: Because my job's in London and my family's in Prague.
A: Who [4] _____ with?
B: I live with my wife and two children in Prague. In London I live alone.
A: What [5] _____?
B: I'm a hotel manager.
A: Where [6] _____?
B: I work in an office in the hotel.

**B** ▶ 4.1 Listen and check.

**C** Underline the stressed words in the questions in Exercise 5A.

*What's your <u>name</u>?*

**D** Listen again and repeat.

## WRITING
### LINKERS AND, BECAUSE

**6** Read the forum entry and cross out the incorrect alternatives.

# Why are you in ...
# Paris?

I'm a student in Paris [1]*and/~~because~~* I study French at university. I'm in France [2]*and/because* my parents work here; my father's a businessman [3]*and/because* my mother's a teacher. I don't live with my parents [4]*and/because* they live in the countryside, 150 km from Paris. I live in a flat in the city [5]*and/because* I walk to the university. I don't have a computer in my flat [6]*and/because* I have a phone with internet, [7]*and/because* I write emails on my phone. I love big cities [8]*and/because* on holiday I always go to cities. I think Paris is a beautiful city [9]*and/because* it has a lot of old buildings, but I don't like the winter [10]*and/because* it's cold.

## GRAMMAR

### PRESENT SIMPLE: HE/SHE/IT

**1 A** Write the *he/she/it* form of the verbs.

1 want _____wants_____
2 do _____
3 teach _____
4 listen _____
5 ask _____
6 stop _____
7 say _____
8 read _____
9 know _____
10 watch _____
11 write _____
12 go _____

**B** ▶ 4.2 Listen and write the verbs from Exercise 1A next to the correct sound.

/s/ _wants,_ _____
/z/ _____
/ɪz/ _____

**2** Look at the pictures and write sentences using the words in brackets ( ).

1 She *doesn't live in Rome. She lives at home* _____. (live)

2 He _____. (play)

3 She _____. (drive)

4 It _____. (cost)

5 He _____. (teach)

6 She _____. (have)

## LISTENING

**3 A** ▶ 4.3 Listen to the radio programme and circle the correct alternative.

The name of the company is Twin Taxi Company because:

**a)** It has two taxis.
**b)** The drivers are twins.
**c)** The company is in Twin City.

**B** Listen again. Are the sentences true (T) or false (F)?

1 Angela and Matt have one taxi. _____
2 Their taxi company is open at night. _____
3 They don't like their job. _____
4 Angela and Matt both have children. _____
5 They're husband and wife. _____
6 They don't see each other. _____

**C** Complete the sentences with the numbers in the box. You don't need two of the numbers.

| ~~11~~ | 26 | 6 | 1 | 17 | 4 | 36 | 2 |
|---|---|---|---|---|---|---|---|

1 Matt drives __11__ hours a day.
2 Angela and Matt are _____ years old.
3 Matt has _____ children.
4 Matt's daughter is _____ years old.
5 Angela's daughter is _____ years old.
6 Angela and Matt have coffee together at _____ in the morning.

**D** Listen again or read audio script 4.3 on page 74 and check.

## VOCABULARY

### DAYS; TIME PHRASES

**4 A** Put the letters in the correct order to make days of the week.

1 Saydun

2 **seaduTy**

3 shuTyard

4 *aidFry*

5 *sandyWeed*

6 **dynaMo**

7 **aSadyurt**

| | |
|---|---|
| 1 _Sunday_ | 5 _____ |
| 2 _____ | 6 _____ |
| 3 _____ | 7 _____ |
| 4 _____ | |

**B** ▶ 4.4 Listen and check.

**C** Listen again and underline the word stress.

**5** Look at the diary and calendar. Write the time phrases.

_Sunday_

**MAY 20th**

| | |
|---|---|
| 8.00 | |
| 9.00 | Dentist |
| 10.00 | |
| 11.00 | |
| 12.00 | |
| 1.00 | |
| 2.00 | |
| 3.00 | Meet Dad |
| 4.00 | |
| 5.00 | |
| 6.00 | |
| 7.00 | Theatre |
| 8.00 | |
| 9.00 | |
| 10.00 | |
| 11.00 | Taxi home |
| 12.00 | |

| MON | TUE | WED | THUR | FRI | SAT | SUN |
|---|---|---|---|---|---|---|
| 1 Coffee with Annick 5pm | 2 | 3 Swim 7pm | 4 | 5 | 6 | 7 |
| 8 | 9 | 10 Swim 7pm | 11 | 12 | 13 | 14 Stay at Grandma's |
| 15 | 16 | 17 Swim 7pm | 18 | 19 | 20 | 21 |
| 22 English class 11-12 | 23 English class 11-12 | 24 English class 11-12 Swim 7pm | 25 English class 11-12 | 26 English class 11-12 | 27 | 28 |
| 29 | 30 | 31 Swim 7pm | | | | |

1 Dentist: _in the morning_
2 Meet Dad: _____
3 Theatre: _____
4 Taxi home: _____
5 Coffee with Annick: _on Monday_
6 Swimming: _____
7 Stay at Grandma's: _____
8 English class: _____

**6 A** Underline the correct alternatives.

1 **A:** When are the English lessons?
  **B:** We meet *in/at/every* Tuesday and Thursday at 7p.m.
2 **A:** See you on Friday!
  **B:** OK. Let's meet *in/at/every* the evening for coffee.
3 **A:** Do you have work this week?
  **B:** Yes, I work *on/at/every* day, and at the weekend, too.
4 **A:** Why are you so tired?
  **B:** I work *in the/at/on* night and go to university *in the/at/on* morning. I don't sleep!
5 **A:** Are you here tomorrow?
  **B:** Yes, I'm here *in/on/every* morning, but not *in/at/on* the afternoon.

**B** ▶ 4.5 Listen and check. Then listen again and say the conversation with the speakers.

# VOCABULARY

## EVENTS

**1 A** Find six words for events.

(match) party festival play concert film

**B** Write the events.

1 It has music: _party_, _____, _____, _____

2 It has actors: _____, _____

3 It has a ball: _____

# FUNCTION

## TELLING THE TIME

**2** Match the times to the clocks.

A

B

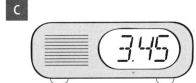
C  3.45

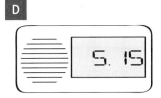
D  5. 15

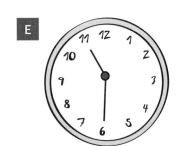
E

F

G  12.30

H

1 half past eleven ___E___     5 half past twelve ____
2 quarter past four ____        6 quarter to four ____
3 six o'clock ____               7 twelve o'clock ____
4 quarter to five ____          8 quarter past five ____

**B** Write the times in words.

1 9.15 _quarter past nine_ _____
2 3.00 _____
3 4.30 _____
4 1.45 _____
5 12.45 _____
6 8.00 _____

**C** ▶ **4.6** Listen and tick (✓) the times you hear.

1 **a)** 1.00 ✓   **b)** 11.00   **c)** 10.00
2 **a)** 5.45     **b)** 6.15    **c)** 5.15
3 **a)** 12.45    **b)** 11.45   **c)** 11.15
4 **a)** 8.30     **b)** 5.30    **c)** 9.30
5 **a)** 6.45     **b)** 3.45    **c)** 6.15
6 **a)** 11.00    **b)** 7.00    **c)** 5.00
7 **a)** 4.15     **b)** 4.45    **c)** 2.15
8 **a)** 3.30     **b)** 2.00    **c)** 2.30

# LEARN TO

## CHECK TIMES

**3 A** Put the sentences in the correct order to make conversations.

**Conversation 1**
a) Half past nine. OK, thanks. _____
b) Half past nine. _____
c) Sorry? _____
d) What time's the football match? __1__
e) The football match? At half past nine. _____

**Conversation 2**
a) At seven? OK. Let's go! _____
b) Maybe. What time does it start? _____
c) Do you want to go to a party? __1__
d) It starts at seven. _____

**B** ▶ **4.7** Listen and check. Then listen again and say the conversation with the speakers.

# VOCABULARY

## EVENTS AND TIMES

**4** Cross out the 'odd one out'.

1 concert/ festival/~~work~~/party
2 quarter past/half past/quarter to/clock
3 afternoon/morning/ten o'clock/night

## GRAMMAR   PRESENT SIMPLE

**1 A** Complete the text with the correct form of the verbs in the box.

> be   say   drive (x2)   do   have (x2)   think
> play (x2)   know   live   ask   watch (x2)

# Actor or doctor?

Vince Chambers ¹ ___is___ an actor, not a doctor. But on TV he's Dr Jenkins, on the TV series *Emergency!*

'I ² _____ (not) about illnesses*,' ³ _____ Chambers. 'But people ⁴ _____ me questions about illnesses all the time. They ⁵ _____ I'm a doctor because I'm a doctor on TV.'

In real life Chambers is very different from his TV character, Dr Jenkins. Dr Jenkins ⁶ _____ a big house, ⁷ _____ a yellow Porsche, and ⁸ _____ golf every weekend. Chambers ⁹ _____ in a big house, but ¹⁰ _____ (not) golf, and he ¹¹ _____ (not) a Porsche. Dr Jenkins ¹² _____ sport every evening, and he ¹³ _____ (not) TV.

'I ¹⁴ _____ (not) time for sport,' says Chambers, 'but I ¹⁵ _____ football on TV every Saturday. But I'm happy. I don't want a Porsche, I don't like golf. And I don't want to be a doctor.'

*\* illness: you have an illness = you are ill.*

**B** Put the words in brackets in the correct place to make questions for Vince Chambers.

1  Are a doctor? (you)
2  Do think you're a doctor? (people)
3  Why do think you're a doctor? (people)
4  Where do live? (you)
5  Do play golf? (you)
6  What do do at the weekend? (you)
7  Are happy? (you)
8  Do want a Porsche? (you)

**C** Write Vince's answers to the questions in Exercise 1B.

1  *No, I'm not. I'm an actor.*
2  _____
3  _____
4  _____
5  _____
6  _____
7  _____
8  _____

## FUNCTION   TELLING THE TIME; ORDERING IN A CAFÉ

**2 A** Put the words of each line in order to make poems (lines 2 and 4 end with the same sound).

**1**
A: it / is / time / What / now?
B: three. / to / quarter / It's
A: have / let's / coffee. / So / a
B: I / Can / a / tea? / have
*What time is it now?*

_____
_____
_____

**2**
A: is / film / eight. / The / at
B: good, / it's / ten! / Oh / at
A: eight! / ten, / Not / at / it's
B: again? / that / you / Can / say

_____
_____
_____
_____

**3**
A: have / I / water? / Can
B: still? / Sparkling / or
A: want / I / I / sparkling. / think very / I / ill. / feel

_____
_____
_____
_____

**4**
A: hungry. / tired / I'm / and
B: let's / break. / have / So / a
A: a / have / Can / coffee? / I
B: cake? / have / I / Can / a

_____
_____
_____
_____

**B** ▶ R2.1 Listen and check. Then listen again and say the poems with the speakers.

**GRAMMAR**  THIS/THAT/THESE/THOSE; POSSESSIVE 'S

**3** Underline the correct alternatives.

**A:** Can I help you, sir?

**B:** Yes, do you have my wife's purse?

**A:** A purse? Just a minute.

**B:** Er … what are ¹*these/those* things there?

**A:** ²*These/Those*? They're keys. About a hundred different keys.

**B:** Wow! And is ³*this/that* a computer over there?

**A:** Yes, it is. And look at ⁴*this/these* purse. A purse with a hundred euros in it.

**B:** Oh, I think ⁵*this/that* 's my wife's purse.

**A:** Ha ha!

**B:** And what ⁶*is/are* those? ⁷*Is/Are* that a clothes box?

**A:** Oh, yes. ⁸*This/These* are hats, about twenty different hats. Do you want a hat?

**B:** No, thanks. What are ⁹*that/those*? Are they watches?

**A:** Yes, ¹⁰*this/these* is a box of watches.

**B:** Do people come for their things?

**A:** Yes, of course. But not ¹¹*these/this* things. They're here for ever, I think.

**B:** Erm … my wife's purse? It's small and black.

**A:** Ah, yes. Is ¹²*this/these* her purse?

**4** Read the notes and complete the information. What is lost?

1 My purse. It has 100 euros in it! (Charlotte)

        *Charlotte's purse*

2 My hat. It's red and very new. (Dan)

 

3 My house keys. Three keys on a key ring. (Tom)

 

4 My computer. All my work is on it. (Bence)

 

5 My leather bag. It's a black woman's bag. (Jean)

 

6 My favourite T-shirt. Blue and white. (Ann Marie)

 

7 My phone. It's an iPhone 5. (Peter)

 

**VOCABULARY**  REVISION

**5** Complete the sentences with words beginning with the letters A–Z.

**A**  I drink coffee in the morning and tea in the ___*afternoon*___ .

**B**  An egg sandwich on ___*brown*___ bread, please.

**C**  I don't go to plays, but I go to _____ .

**D**  Monday, Tuesday, Wednesday are all _____ .

**E**  He works in the afternoon, but not in the _____ .

**F**  Is the film on Thursday or _____ ?

**G**  It's very cold. Do you have your _____ ?

**H**  Half the students don't do their _____ .

**I**  **A:** Let's go to the festival.
    **B:** Good _____ !

**J**  How much is that black _____ ?

**K**  Where are my car _____ ?

**L**  I don't _____ with my parents. I have a flat in the city.

**M**  What time is the football _____ ?

**N**  We read the _____ online, not in a newspaper.

**O**  Greg works in an _____ in Moscow.

**P**  It's Sonya's birthday _____ today.

**Q**  The film is at _____ to eight.

**R**  I like that _____ and white T-shirt.

**S**  The day before Sunday is _____ .

**T**  Black skirt, black shoes and black _____ – very nice!

**U**  What do you study at _____ ?

**V**  The words *be* and *live* are _____ .

**W**  We have classes on _____ mornings.

**X**  Work in pairs and do e_____ 4B.

**Y**  My favourite colour is _____ .

**Z**  My car goes from _____ to sixty in ten seconds.

## CHECK

Circle the correct option to complete the sentences.

1  Excuse me, _____ is my bag.
   a) this
   b) that's
   c) those

2  The _____ is hot!
   a) business card
   b) coffee
   c) keys

3  _____ English?
   a) Speak you
   b) Do you speak
   c) Do you speak the

4  Let's _____ Greece.
   a) go
   b) go in
   c) go to

5  Are _____ your books?
   a) this
   b) those
   c) thise

6  A: What time is it?
   B: It's _____ eleven.
   a) half past
   b) half to
   c) one half

7  _____ is blue.
   a) Michael's hat
   b) Michael hat's
   c) Michael his hat

8  She _____ English.
   a) studies not
   b) doesn't study
   c) doesn't studies

9  _____ a coffee, please?
   a) Can I
   b) I can have
   c) Can I have

10  Look! The water is a beautiful _____ colour!
   a) brown
   b) blue
   c) yellow

11  A: I'm cold!
    B: Oh, here's my _____.
    a) sweater
    b) T-shirt
    c) trousers

12  What's _____ phone number?
    a) Tesses
    b) Tess her
    c) Tess's

13  The _____ is in the _____.
    a) printers, car
    b) clock, table
    c) picture, box

14  Is it quarter _____ or quarter _____ three?
    a) past, to
    b) half, to
    c) past, at

15  A: A mineral water, please.
    B: Still _____?
    a) or sparkling
    b) or please
    c) and sparkling

16  They _____ in an office.
    a) not work
    b) no work
    c) don't work

17  The day after Monday is _____.
    a) Thursday
    b) Tuesday
    c) Sunday

18  We go to a café _____ morning.
    a) in
    b) at
    c) every

19  George _____ a car.
    a) has
    b) haves
    c) haz

20  I live _____.
    a) with my family
    b) a car
    c) in house

RESULT          /20

## VOCABULARY

### DAILY ROUTINES

**1 A** Put the letters in the correct order to make phrases about daily routines. The first letter is underlined.

1 <u>p</u>egtu     _get up_
2 <u>i</u>nvaderhen     _____
3 <u>h</u>unchveal     _____
4 <u>g</u>oodbet     _____
5 <u>v</u>astfakere<u>ha</u>b     _____
6 <u>m</u>eethog     _____
7 <u>t</u>ookgrow     _____

**B** Number the verbs in order of time of day.

_get up 1_

## READING

**2 A** Read the text. Which actions are in the picture?

### An English teacher writes ...
#### 10 things that drive me crazy

I love my job. I really like teaching English and my students are great. But sometimes they drive me crazy! I don't like it when a student:

1 comes to the class late every day.
2 talks on his or her phone or sends texts in the lesson.
3 doesn't finish the homework, or doesn't do it.
4 has food or drink in the lesson.
5 looks at his or her computer all the time.
6 listens to his or her smartphone in the lesson.
7 doesn't answer my question but only looks at me.
8 speaks his or her language and doesn't speak English.
9 looks in his or her dictionary twenty times in the lesson.
10 comes to class ill or tired.

Are you a student? Do you do these things?
Maybe you drive your teacher crazy!

**B** Who says these sentences? The teacher (T) or a student (S)?

a) 'Where is your homework, Wu?'    _T_
b) _'No entiendo.'_    _S_
c) 'Are you OK, Janine? You don't look well.'    _____
d) 'Please close that. You don't understand a word? Please ask me.'    _____
e) 'Hi, Estella. It's me. Shhh. I'm in class.'    _____
f) 'Chris? Chris? CHRIS! Listen to me, not your music. Thank you.'    _____
g) 'The lesson starts at nine o'clock, Jamal, not half past nine.'    _____
h) 'But I'm thirsty.'    _____

**C** Match the sentences in Exercise 2B with eight of sentences 1–10 in the text.

a) _3_    b) _____    c) _____
d) _____    e) _____    f) _____
g) _____    h) _____

**D** Read the text again and complete the sentences in the positive (+) or negative (–).

A good student of English:

1 _doesn't speak_ in his or her language in the class.
2 _____ the homework.
3 _____ to the class early.
4 _____ food in the class.
5 _____ cola in the class.
6 _____ to the teacher and not to a smartphone.
7 _____ texts in class.
8 _____ the teacher questions in class.

# GRAMMAR

## PRESENT SIMPLE QUESTIONS: HE/SHE/IT

**3 A** Look at the teacher's notes about Calvin. Is Calvin a good student, do you think?

### Calvin Cavalieri

1  comes to class on time (at nine o'clock) ✓
2  asks questions in class ✓
3  listens to the answers ✗
4  speaks English in class ✗
5  writes in the class blog ✓
6  reads English books ✗
7  watches films in English ✓
8  does his homework ✗

**B** Write questions about Calvin.

1  *Does Calvin come to class on time?*
2  *Does he ...*
3  _____
4  _____
5  _____
6  _____
7  _____
8  _____

**C** Cover the text and write short answers to the questions in Exercise 3B. Then read the text again and check.

1  *Yes, he does.*
2  _____
3  _____
4  _____
5  _____
6  _____
7  _____
8  _____

**D** ▶ 5.1 Look at the different pronunciation of *does* in the question and the short answer. Then listen to questions 1–8 and repeat.

Does Calvin come to class on time?
/dəz/
Yes, he does.
/dʌz/

**4 A** Look at the table and complete the questions about Maria.

| | Maria, working mother | Nadja, Maria's daughter |
|---|---|---|
| |  |  |
| gets up | at 7a.m. every day | at 8a.m. in the week and at 11a.m. at the weekend |
| in the morning | has coffee and makes a sandwich for Nadja's lunch | reads her emails and has coffee |
| after breakfast | goes to work | goes to school |
| all day | works in a bank | goes to classes |
| friends | meets her friends for tea after work | meets her friends at a café after school |
| in the evening | watches the news on TV | plays games on the internet or phones her boyfriend |
| goes to bed | at 10p.m. in the week and at 12a.m. at the weekend | at 11.45p.m. on school nights and at 1a.m. at the weekend |

1  When _____*does*_____ she _____*get up*_____ ?
   At 7a.m.
2  What _____ she _____ in the morning?
   Coffee.
3  What _____ she _____ for Nadja's lunch?
   A sandwich.
4  Where _____ she _____ after breakfast?
   To work.
5  Who _____ she _____ in the afternoon?
   Her friends.
6  What _____ she _____ on TV in the evening?
   The news.
7  What time _____ she _____ to bed at the weekend?
   At 12a.m.

**B** Look at the answers and write the questions about Nadja.

1  *When does Nadja get up at the weekend?*
   At 11a.m.
2  _____
   Her emails.
3  _____
   To school.
4  _____
   At a café.
5  _____
   She plays games on the internet.
6  _____
   Her boyfriend.
7  _____
   At 11.45p.m.

# VOCABULARY

## FOOD

**1 A** Look at the pictures. Find eight kinds of food.

| P | A | S | T | A | E | C | L | O | B |
|---|---|---|---|---|---|---|---|---|---|
| E | D | T | A | F | G | H | A | D | I |
| F | E | E | H | M | P | E | S | Y | S |
| U | C | A | J | K | L | E | T | C | C |
| R | I | K | S | F | I | S | H | H | U |
| I | M | R | B | A | R | E | D | T | I |
| C | H | I | C | K | E | N | A | N | T |
| E | D | S | N | L | O | E | G | G | S |

**1 B** Add *a, e, i* or *u* to make food names.

1 fr*u*_*i*t
2 v_g_t_bl_s
3 p_zz_
4 m_lk
5 l_tt_c_

# GRAMMAR

## ADVERBS OF FREQUENCY

**2 A** Complete the adverbs of frequency.

100%    **1** _____always_____

       **2** u_____

       **3** o_____

       **4** s_____

       **5** no_____ o_____

0%    **6** n_____

**B** Look at the information about a woman's lifestyle in the month of May. Do you think she is a dancer or a doctor?

| gets up at eight | 31 days |
|---|---|
| has breakfast | 0 days |
| does sport in the morning | 9 days |
| eats pizza | 2 days |
| drinks water with her lunch | 28 days |
| works in the evening | 23 days |
| is hungry at night | 31 days |

**C** Write sentences about the woman. Use adverbs of frequency.

1 *She always gets up at eight.* _____
2 _____
3 _____
4 _____
5 _____
6 _____
7 _____

**3** Add the adverbs in brackets to the sentences.

1 He's hungry because he eats a lot. (never, always)
   *He's never hungry because he always eats a lot.*

2 I go to bed late and I'm tired. (often, usually)
   _____

3 They have money, but they're happy. (not often, always)
   _____

4 We study for the test, but we get 100%. (never, usually)
   _____

5 It's hot here, but it's very cold. (not often, never)
   _____

6 She gets home late, but she has dinner with her family. (sometimes, always)
   _____

## LISTENING

# Radio You:
### What do you eat? 11a.m.

At 180 kilograms, many people ask George Palakiko 'How do you do it? How are you so big?' Today on *What do you eat?* we talk to Palakiko in person and get surprising answers to these questions.

**4 A** Read the programme information. Do you think sentences 1–6 are true (T) or false (F)?

1 He's from Japan. _____
2 He doesn't have breakfast. _____
3 He does sumo training in the morning. _____
4 He eats junk food (pizza, hamburgers). _____
5 He drinks beer. _____
6 He sleeps in the afternoon. _____

**B** ▶ 5.2 Listen to the programme and check your answers.

**C** Listen again. What do the numbers mean?

a) 7 *He gets up at 7.* _____
b) 12 _____
c) 6 _____
d) 4 _____
e) 10 _____

**D** Listen again and underline the correct alternatives.

1 Everyone *asks/has* that question.
2 What's a *typical/usual* day?
3 I'm *very/never* hungry in the mornings.
4 We *have/eat* lunch together.
5 It's *a/with* chicken, *dish/fish* and vegetables.
6 Let's *go to/have* lunch.

## WRITING

### LINKERS TO SEQUENCE

**5 A** What is your perfect weekend? Underline the correct alternatives for you.

1 I get up *early/late/the same time as in the week*.
2 I do things *alone/with my friends/with my family*.
3 I *go to the countryside/go to the city/stay at home*.

**B** Read about Sally's perfect weekend. Is it the same or different from your perfect weekend? Tick (✓) the things that are the same.

## My perfect **weekend**
*(by Sally)*

1 _____First_____ on Saturday I don't get up. I sleep all day. 2 _____ I get up at six in the evening and have breakfast. I make a tea and go online. 3 _____ that I go to a party or I go to bed. 4 _____ on Sunday I get up at ten or eleven o'clock. My friends come to my flat and we talk. 5 _____ that we go out and walk, but not very far. 6 _____ we have dinner in a nice restaurant.

**C** Complete the text in Exercise 5B with the linkers in the box.

| Finally   ~~First~~   After (x2)   Then (x2) |

**D** Add four commas (,) to the text.

**6** Write about your perfect weekend (60–80 words).

_____

_____

_____

_____

_____

_____

_____

_____

_____

_____

_____

# VOCABULARY

## HOTEL SERVICES

**1 A** Where are the people? Complete the crossword with the hotel services.

**Across**

3 'Is that the Sydney Opera House?'
4 'Can I have dollars, please?'
6 'Do you have postcards?'
7 'Can I have steak and vegetables, please?'

**Down**

1 'Come in! The water's lovely!'
2 'A haircut, please.'
3 'I don't have my trainers. Are these shoes OK?'
5 'Can I have one of those cakes and a coffee, please?'

**B** What's the word stress? Put the words from the crossword in the correct place in the table.

| ¹O |
|---|
| |
| ²Oo |
| |
| ³Ooo |
| |
| ⁴OoO |
| *guided tour* |
| ⁵OooO |
| |

**C** ▶ 5.3 Listen and check. Then listen and repeat.

# FUNCTION

## ASKING FOR INFORMATION

> # Guided tour of the city
>
> ( Every hour from 10a.m. ) ――― 1
> ――― 2
> Ticket office open ( 9a.m. ) – ( 5p.m. )
> ――― 3
> ( 25 euros )
> ――― 4
> Bus leaves ( from ticket office )
> ――― 5

**2 A** Look at the information and write the questions.

1 When *does the guided tour leave* _____?
2 What time _____?
3 When _____?
4 How much _____?
5 Where _____ from?

**B** ▶ 5.4 Listen and check.

**C** Listen again and write one piece of extra information for each question.

1 *There's isn't a guided tour at five today.*
2 _____
_____
3 _____
_____
4 _____
_____
5 _____
_____

# LEARN TO

## USE TWO-PART EXCHANGES

**3 A** ▶ 5.5 Listen to three conversations. Which phrase in the box is <u>not</u> in the conversations?

> That's a shame.   Great.   You're welcome.
> You too.   Right.   Thank you.

**B** Listen again. Match 1–5 with responses a–e.

1 Can I help you?　　　　a) You're welcome.
2 … I'm sorry.　　　　　b) Yes. What time is lunch?
3 Yes, we do.　　　　　c) Right. Thank you.
4 It opens at 10 and
　closes at 4.　　　　　d) That's a shame.
5 Great. Thanks.　　　　e) Great.

## VOCABULARY

### PLACES

**1 A** Find eight places. Some places are in two parts. One word appears twice.

| P | H | A | R | M | A | C | Y | I | M |
|---|---|---|---|---|---|---|---|---|---|
| R | E | S | T | A | U | R | A | N | T |
| G | P | O | C | G | C | T | K | T | A |
| M | W | I | A | P | H | O | N | E | C |
| A | F | X | F | L | K | L | W | R | A |
| C | W | Z | E | S | A | M | R | N | S |
| H | O | T | E | L | T | B | L | E | H |
| I | W | N | I | A | G | E | N | T | S |
| N | C | A | F | E | C | N | E | W | S |
| E | A | F | E | P | A | Y | F | L | I |

**B** Match the sentences with places in the puzzle.

1 You have a sandwich and a drink in this place.

   _café_

2 You write an email and have a coffee here.

3 You get a room for the night here.

4 You phone a friend from here.

5 You buy a newspaper here.

6 You put your card in and take your money out here.

7 You have a good dinner here.

8 Are you ill? Go to this place.

**C** ▶ 6.1 Listen and check. Then listen again and answer the questions.

1 Which places have two syllables?

   _café, …_

2 Which places have three or more syllables?

   _internet café, …_

## GRAMMAR

### THERE IS/ARE

**2** Write the sentences.

1 ✓ cafés   ✗ internet cafés

   _There are cafés, but there aren't any internet cafés._

2 ✓ cash machine   ✗ money exchange

3 ✓ restaurant   ✗ waiters

4 ✗ buses   ✓ taxis

5 ✗ computer   ✓ printer

6 ✓ five men   ✗ women

**3** Write questions for places 1–8. Then look at the picture and write short answers.

1 snack bar

   _Is there a café?_                    _Yes, there is._

2 internet café

3 payphones

4 cash machines

5 newsagent's

6 toilets

7 hairdresser's

8 clock

## READING

**4 A** Look at the photo. Do you think the train station is in Tibet, the USA, Spain, Turkey or England?

**B** Read the article and check.

# No trains? *Great!*

**People don't usually like waiting in train stations.
They feel bored, and there's nothing interesting to see or do.
But that's not true in these train stations!**

**1** Tanggula Mountain Railway Station, Tibet, is at 5,058 metres. The Tanggula mountains and the river are a beautiful sight. It's a lovely place to wait for a train.

**2** Union Station in Washington DC, USA, is the number one place for many tourists. It's over 100 years old, there are 130 shops, and many restaurants and cafés. The station is a great place to bring your family for a dinner, and people never feel bored – there's so much to do and see.

**3** Atocha Station in Madrid, Spain, has trees inside the station, so people walk around and drink coffee in the middle of a beautiful green jungle.

**4** Haydarpasa Station in Istanbul, Turkey, is almost an island. It stands in the sea, and has water on three sides. There are boats from the station.

**5** Pickering Station in Yorkshire, England, is a small town station with an old-time atmosphere. There's a hairdresser's and an old tea room. Once a year the people there dress in 1940s clothes.

**C** Read the article again and match headings a)–e) with paragraphs 1–5.

**a)** Beautiful views _____1_____

**b)** Shop and eat all day _____

**c)** No train? Take a boat! _____

**d)** What year is it now? _____

**e)** Green all around _____

**D** Read the article again. What is the same about:

**1** stations 3 and 4? *They are both in cities.*

**2** stations 1 and 4? _____

**3** stations 2 and 5? _____

## WRITING

### STARTING AND ENDING AN EMAIL

**5 A** Look at the sentences from emails. How many emails are there?

Regards,

Hi Lesley,

My computer is big, my desk is small and my office is cold.

Are you free on Friday evening?

Jim

Derrick Jameson

Please get me a small computer, a big desk and a new sweater.

See you soon,

Is 8 o'clock OK?

Let's have dinner at the Chinese restaurant.

Dear Ms Clements,

I am happy in my job, but there's a problem.

**B** Write W (work email) or F (email to a friend) next to each line above.

| Regards, | *W* |
| Hi Lesley, | *F* |

**C** Write the emails in full.

**1** Hi Lesley, _____

_____

_____

_____

_____

_____

_____

_____

**2** Dear Ms Clements, _____

_____

_____

_____

_____

_____

_____

_____

_____

# VOCABULARY

## TRANSPORT

**1 A** Find eight transport words.

taxi plane train car motor bike bus bike underground

**B** Look at the pictures and write the correct words from Exercise 1A.

1 _____taxi_____

2 _____

3 _____

4 _____

5 _____

6 _____

7 _____

8 _____

# LISTENING

**2 A** ▶ 6.2 Listen to three conversations. Which places a)–e) are the speakers in?

a) a bus
b) an underground train
c) a plane
d) a car
e) a taxi

Conversation 1: _____
Conversation 2: _____
Conversation 3: _____

**B** Listen again and underline the correct alternatives.

**Conversation 1**
a) They want <u>North</u>/South Street.
b) They're from *New York/New Zealand*.
c) They *know/don't know* Belfast.

**Conversation 2**
d) He wants a *black/white* coffee.
e) It's *2.45/3.15* in Moscow.
f) It's *hot/not hot* in Moscow.

**Conversation 3**
g) She wants to go to *Summer Street/ Old Street*.
h) She is with *two/three* children.
i) The café is *five/nine* stops.

**C** Listen again and underline the correct alternatives.

1 **A:** Do you *want/<u>have</u>* any bags?
   **B:** Yes, these, but they're *fine/OK* here.
2 **A:** Yes, the Garden *Hotel/Restaurant*.
   **B:** Right, I *like/know* it.
3 We're on holiday here for *two/three* weeks.
4 And do you *read/know* about the weather?
5 Enjoy your *drink/food*.
6 Do you go to the *town/city* centre?
7 That's two *fifty/sixty*.
8 I don't *know/like* the town.

# GRAMMAR
## A/AN, SOME, A LOT OF, NOT ANY

**3** Complete the sentences with the correct form of *be* and *a/an, some, a lot of* or *not any*.

1 Emails?
There ___'s an___ internet café on our top floor.

2 Good local transport.
There _____ _____ buses and an underground.

3 There _____ _____ tourists – you have a private beach!

4 There _____ _____ friendly money exchange on every street.

5 A: _____ there _____ tourist information centre in town?
B: No, but there _____ information centre here in the hotel.

6 Romantic dinners!
There _____ _____ lovely old restaurants near the sea.

**4 A** Underline the correct alternatives in the conversations.

**Conversation 1**

A: Can I have ¹*a/an* coffee and ²*a/some* cakes, please?
B: Sorry, we don't have ³*some/any* cakes.
A: What? But this sign says 'cakes'.
B: Yes, but there are ⁴*some/a lot of* people here today.
A: OK, can I have ⁵*a/an* egg sandwich then?

**Conversation 2**

A: Excuse me. I don't speak Spanish. Do you have ⁶*a/any* newspapers in English?
B: Yes, there's ⁷*a/an* American newspaper here, but it's from yesterday.
A: You don't have ⁸*a/an* English newspaper?
B: No, we usually have ⁹*some/an* English newspapers, but not today.

**Conversation 3**

A: Hello, I want to study English and I have ¹⁰*a/some* questions.
B: OK.
A: Are there ¹¹*any/a lot of* students in the classes?
B: No, we have small classes – only twelve students in a class. There aren't ¹²*some/any* big classes.

**B** Where are the conversations in Exercise 4A?

1 _____
2 _____
3 _____

**5 A** Put the words in the box in the correct places in the sentences. You don't need to use one of the words.

| ~~of~~  a  an  aren't  any  some (x2) |
|---|

*of*
1 There are a lot ⋀ words on this page.

2 Words on this page have four letters.

3 There are names of people on the page.

4 There any words with twelve letters.

5 This sentence doesn't have letter 'B' in it.

6 There aren't numbers on the page.

**B** Tick (✓) the sentences that are true.

## VOCABULARY
### TRAVEL

**1 A** Add vowels to complete the words.

1 s_i_ngl_e_ t_i_cke_t_
2 t_ck_t __ff_c_
3 r_t_rn t_ck_t
4 p_ss_ng_r
5 m__nthly p_ss
6 g_t_

**B** ▶ 6.3 Listen and check.

**C** Listen again and count the number of syllables. Where's the main stress?

*1 Four: single ticket*

## FUNCTION
### BUYING A TICKET

**2 A** Correct ten mistakes in the conversation.

> to
A: A ticket ~~in~~ Canberra, please.

B: Single and return?

A: Return, please.

B: For today?

A: Sorry, no, on tomorrow.

B: What do you want to go?

A: At afternoon.

B: And when you do want to come back?

A: On Friday, when the morning.

B: OK, that eighty-three dollars.

A: When time's the bus?

B: There's one at quarter to nine.

A: When does it arrive for Canberra?

B: At quarter to eleven.

A: Thanks a lot.

**B** ▶ 6.4 Listen and check.

## LEARN TO
### CHECK NUMBERS

**3 A** Complete the conversations. Write the number in words and underline the stress.

1 A: It's bus number 39.
 B: Sorry? 29?
 A: *No, thirty-nine.*
2 A: That's 49 euros.
 B: Sorry? 45?
 A: _____.
3 A: The plane leaves from gate 58.
 B: Sorry? Gate 88?
 A: _____.
4 A: The bus leaves at 5.15.
 B: Sorry? 4.45?
 A: _____.
5 A: I'm 54 years old.
 B: Sorry, 64?
 A: _____.

**B** ▶ 6.5 Listen and check. Then listen again and repeat.

## VOCABULARY
### TRANSPORT

**4 A** Complete the table with the words in the box.

| train | single | monthly pass | car | ticket office |
| ~~gate~~ | return | platform | station | plane | bus |

| places | type of ticket | ways of travelling |
|---|---|---|
| *gate* | | |

**4 B** Complete the conversation with words from Exercise 4A.

A: A ticket to Dresden, please.
B: ¹ _Single_ or ² _____?
A: A single, please.
B: Forty-one euros, please.
A: Thanks. What time does the ³ _____ leave?
B: Ten o' clock.
A: Which ⁴ _____?
B: Number 2.

## VOCABULARY REVISION

**1 A** Write the correct spelling.

| | | |
|---|---|---|
| 1 | undergrund | _underground_ |
| 2 | busses | |
| 3 | vedgtables | |
| 4 | gided tour | |
| 5 | have brekfast | |
| 6 | chiken | |
| 7 | go to beed | |
| 8 | moterbikes | |
| 9 | tiket office | |
| 10 | biscits | |
| 11 | swiming pool | |
| 12 | newagent's | |
| 13 | have diner | |
| 14 | pessenger | |

**B** Write words from Exercise 1A which can complete the sentences. Use each word once only.

1 The _____ is very expensive!
  _underground,_ _____ _____

2 What time do you _____?
  _____ _____ _____

3 There's a _____ in the station.
  _____ _____ _____

4 I often eat _____.
  _____ _____ _____

5 There are cars and _____ in the street.
  _____ _____

## GRAMMAR PRESENT SIMPLE QUESTIONS: HE/SHE/IT; ADVERBS OF FREQUENCY

**2 A** Read paragraph 1 of the text and choose the best headline.

a) I WATCH PASSENGERS

b) ARE YOU A BAD PASSENGER?

c) 99 PASSENGERS A DAY

**B** Complete the questions about the bad passenger.

1 _Does he have_ a lot of bags? (have)
2 _____ about the bus times? (where/ask)
3 _____ at the café? (what/do)
4 _____ in the station? (what/read)
5 _____ to the bus? (when/get)
6 _____ his ticket? (where/have)
7 _____ on the bus? (what/eat)
8 _____ thank you? (say)

**1** My name's Eric Roamer. I'm a bus driver. I love my job and 99 out of 100 passengers are great, but number 100 is THE BAD PASSENGER. You see him in the bus station and you know him. How do you know? It's easy. Watch him buy a ticket. Watch him at the café. And watch him on the bus.

**2** He doesn't go to the information desk. He goes to the ticket office and asks questions about the bus times, with people waiting behind him. In the café he reads the menu for ten minutes and then he gets a coffee. In the bus station he reads a newspaper, but not his newspaper – another passenger's newspaper. He doesn't buy newspapers.

**3** The bus leaves at ten. The bad passenger gets to the bus at one minute to ten, usually with four bags. But where's his ticket? It's in a bag, but there are four bags and he doesn't know which one. He finds his ticket, after five minutes. So 7 times out of 10, the bus leaves late.

**4** On the bus he often eats fast food and chocolate and then he leaves the paper on the seat. And of course, at the end of the journey, he never says thank you. He says, 'It's too hot on the bus,' or 'It's too cold,' or 'We're late.' I say, 'Have a nice day!'

**C** Read paragraphs 2–4 and answer the questions in Exercise 2B.

1 _Yes, he does._
2 _____
3 _____
4 _____
5 _____
6 _____
7 _____
8 _____

**D** Read the text again. Then complete the sentences with the correct adverb in brackets.

  _n't often_
1 There are ∧ bad passengers on buses. (not often/never)

2 The bad passenger asks questions at the information desk. (usually/never)

3 He asks questions at the ticket office. (always/sometimes)

4 He has a lot of bags. (usually/not often)

5 The bus is late because of the bad passenger. (often/never)

6 He says, 'It's hot on the bus.' (sometimes/always)

## FUNCTION — ASKING FOR INFORMATION AND BUYING A TICKET

**3 A** Match jobs 1–3 with information A–C.

1 train ticket office assistant
2 tourist information assistant
3 hotel receptionist

---

**A** **Restaurant meal times**

Breakfast: [1]_____ to [2]_____

Lunch: [3]_____ to [4]_____

Dinner: [5]_____ to [6]_____

**You're welcome for coffee and desserts between meals!**

---

**B** **Tourist Information**

**Old town bus tour:**

[7]_____, 1.30, [8]_____

Price: [9]_____

**Summer theatre in the park:**

**Monday:** Concert at [10]_____p.m.

Price: [11]_____

**Tuesday:** Theatre at [12]_____p.m.

Price: [13]_____

---

**C** TICKET

**Return ticket**

London to Brighton

Departure: [14]_____ o'clock

Price: [15]_____

---

**B**  R3.1 Listen to the conversations and complete the information in A–C.

**C** Complete the questions with two words.

1 Is _____ *there a* _____ café in the hotel?
2 _____ the restaurant open for dinner?
3 What _____ it leave?
4 How _____ it cost?
5 _____ the next train to Brighton?
6 _____ you want to come back?

**D** ▶ R3.2 Listen and check. Then listen and say the conversations with the speakers.

---

## GRAMMAR — *THERE IS/ARE; A/AN, SOME, A LOT OF, NOT ANY*

**4 A** Underline the correct alternatives.

### Travellers' Tips:

## Sicily in January

Eight reasons why it's a good time to go.

1 There *are/aren't* any people on the beach in January. In summer there *is/are* a lot of people, and it's very noisy.

2 Yes, the beach is cold, but *some/any* hotels have swimming pools.

3 There are *a lot/a lot of* empty hotel rooms.

4 Some hotels *has/have* low prices in winter.

5 It's not hot in winter. Summer is very hot – on *some/lot of* days it's over 40°C.

6 On every street there's *a/an* Italian restaurant with great pasta and *a/an* friendly waiter.

7 There's/*are* snow on Mount Etna – great for skiing!

8 There's *a/some* golf course and it's not expensive in winter.

---

**B** Complete the tourist's questions about transport in Sicily.

1 _____ *Is there* _____ a train from Palermo airport to the city centre?
2 _____ taxis from the airport?
3 _____ an underground in Palermo?
4 _____ buses in Palermo?
5 _____ a plane from Palermo to Rome every day?
6 _____ roads for bikes?

**C** Match answers a)–f) with questions 1–6 in Exercise 4B.

a) Yes, there is. They call it the metro. _____3_____

b) Yes, there is. There are also buses from Palermo to Rome. _____

c) Yes, there are, but they cost a lot of money. Take the bus. _____

d) I don't know, but there are a lot of cars on the main roads, so it's dangerous. _____

e) Yes, there is. There are buses and taxis to the centre of Palermo, too. _____

f) Yes, there are. A twenty-four hour bus ticket is four euros. _____

## CHECK

Circle the correct option to complete the sentences.

**1** When _____ get up?
- **a)** does she
- **b)** she does
- **c)** she

**2** I _____ late.
- **a)** 'm never
- **b)** never am
- **c)** never

**3** Look at this big, red _____!
- **a)** bread
- **b)** cereal
- **c)** apple

**4** _____ a cash machine near here?
- **a)** Is there
- **b)** Does there
- **c)** Are there

**5** Postcards? The _____ is over there.
- **a)** hairdresser's
- **b)** gift shop
- **c)** gym

**6** What time does it _____ Kyoto?
- **a)** go in
- **b)** arrive in
- **c)** get in

**7** He doesn't have _____ water.
- **a)** some
- **b)** no
- **c)** any

**8 A:** Does your brother live in London?
**B:** Yes, _____.
- **a)** he lives.
- **b)** he does.
- **c)** he does live.

**9 A:** A _____ ticket, please.
**B:** When do you want to come back?
- **a)** return
- **b)** single
- **c)** monthly

**10** I get _____ at 7 and have _____.
- **a)** up, breakfast
- **b)** home, bed
- **c)** work, lunch

**11** Are there _____ English people in the class?
- **a)** a lot of
- **b)** an
- **c)** some of

**12 A:** Thank you.
**B:** You're _____.
- **a)** OK
- **b)** welcome
- **c)** regards

**13** _____ does the tour cost?
- **a)** When
- **b)** What time
- **c)** How much

**14** There _____ any cafés in the town.
- **a)** isn't
- **b)** aren't
- **c)** are

**15** We _____ dinner at home.
- **a)** have usually
- **b)** usually
- **c)** usually have

**16 A:** I'm thirsty.
**B:** There's a _____ over there.
- **a)** pharmacy
- **b)** café
- **c)** cash machine

**17** _____ at two.
- **a)** It opens
- **b)** Its opens
- **c)** It costs

**18** What time do you _____ home?
- **a)** go to
- **b)** get
- **c)** get to

**19** Look! There are about a hundred people on that _____.
- **a)** motorbike
- **b)** car
- **c)** bus

**20** A single _____ Chang Mai _____ tomorrow, please.
- **a)** for, to
- **b)** to, to
- **c)** to, for

| RESULT | /20 |
| --- | --- |

# GRAMMAR

## PAST SIMPLE: WAS/WERE

**1 A** Match emails 1–3 with replies a)–c).

1 ___c___   2 _____   3 _____

---

**1**

Hi Larissa,

Sorry you weren't at my birthday lunch yesterday. The weather was beautiful so lunch was in the garden. Where were you?

Mark

**2**

Hi George,

Where were you and Maria yesterday? It was my birthday lunch, at Mum and Dad's house. Remember?

Mark

**3**

Hi Diana,

I was really happy that you and Alan were at my birthday lunch yesterday. It was great to see you and the children.

Mark

---

**a)**

Mark,

So sorry. We were in Spain on holiday, but we're home now. Happy 30th birthday!

**b)**

Hi Mark,

Thank you for the party. It was really nice. Your parents are lovely people, and their garden is lovely, too!

**c)**

Happy birthday one day late! Sorry, I was in London on business. Let's meet soon!

---

**B** Put the words in the correct order to make questions.

1 Mark / Was / twenty?
   *Was Mark twenty?*

2 house? / Mark's / the / lunch / Was / at
   _____

3 lunch? / the / Was / Diana / at
   _____

4 the / and / children / Alan's / at / Were / lunch / Diana?
   _____

5 France? / George / Maria / in / Were / and
   _____

6 weather / the / Was / good?
   _____

**C** Write short answers to the questions in Exercise 2A.

1 ___No, he wasn't.___
2 _____
3 _____
4 _____
5 _____
6 _____

**D** Look at the answers and write the questions. Use the underlined words to help.

1 *Where was the lunch?*
   The lunch was at Mark's parents' house.

2 _____
   Mark's birthday was yesterday.

3 _____
   Mark was thirty.

4 _____
   George and Maria were in Spain.

5 _____
   The lunch was in the garden because it was good weather.

**2** Write the sentences about Mark's party last year. Use the information in brackets.

1 It's my thirtieth birthday. (29th)
   Last year *it was my 29th birthday* .

2 We're here. (not here)
   Last year _____ .

3 My wife's in London on business. (Tokyo on business)
   Last year _____ .

4 Larissa's parents aren't here. (not here)
   Last year _____ .

5 George and Maria are in Spain. (Greece)
   Last year _____ .

6 It's a small party. (big)
   Last year _____ .

7 The weather's beautiful. (terrible)
   Last year _____ .

8 Lunch is in the garden. (in the house)
   Last year _____ .

**7 PAST**

## READING

**3 A** Read the text and match headings 1–5 with paragraphs A–E.

1 Technology _____E_____
2 Family _____
3 Women _____
4 Transport _____
5 Population _____

# A **hundred** years of change

### A

Life in the year 2000 was very different from life in 1900. In ¹ _____1900_____ in the USA, there were three and a half children in an average family. The top boy's name was John and the top girl's name was Mary. In ² _____, the top names were Jacob and Emily and there was only one child in each family.

### B

In ³ _____, there were 54 million new cars on the roads. In ⁴ _____, there were only 4,000 new cars. In cities transport was by horse and a small number of buses.

### C

The number of people in cities was very different. London was the top city in ⁵ _____ with 6 million people. The top city in ⁶ _____ was Tokyo with 27 million people.

### D

Women's lives were very different both at home and in public. For example, in the ⁷ _____ Olympics there were 827 women and 1,512 men, but in ⁸ _____ there were 1,319 men and only 19 women.

### E

⁹ _____ was the year of the Kodak Brownie camera. Letters were the only way to communicate except for telephones in some rich families. In ¹⁰ _____, email was big and there were mobile phones with cameras.

**B** Read the text again and complete the information with *1900* or *2000*.

## VOCABULARY

### DATES

**4 A** Write the dates in words.

a) 2nd Apr _____*the second of April*_____
b) 11th Aug _____
c) 25th Dec _____
d) 8th Mar _____
e) 10th Jun _____
f) 1st Jan _____
g) 31st Oct _____
h) 1st May _____
i) 14th Feb _____
j) 4th Jul _____

**B** Number the dates in the correct order.

**C** ▶ 7.1 Match the holidays with the dates from Exercise 4A. Then listen and check.

1 New Year's Day _____*f*_____
2 Valentine's Day _____
3 May Day _____
4 Independence Day (USA) _____
5 International Women's Day _____
6 Son and Daughter's Day _____
7 Christmas Day _____
8 Children's Day _____
9 Children's Book Day _____
10 Halloween _____

## WRITING

### PUNCTUATION REVIEW

**5 A** Correct the texts. Use four full stops (.), three commas (,), one question mark (?) and one exclamation mark (!).

World Hello Day is on 21st november every year Say 'hello' to ten people on the bus on the train at work at school and in the street. try it this year It's so easy

In the USA, the Sunday after 7th September is grandparents' Day. it's a great day to visit your grandparents or to go out with them why Because they're <u>your</u> grandparents

**B** Change five letters to capital letters.

*21st of ~~november~~*     *November*

**C** Write about a special day in your country.

_____
_____
_____
_____
_____

# VOCABULARY

## ACTIONS

**1 A** Read the clues and complete the crossword.

```
        1
        T
    2       
        R
        A
    3       
        V
        E
    4       5
        L
    6   7
        
        
8       
        
        
9       
```

**Across**

2 I _____ new food every day.
3 We _____ home every year.
4 Do you _____ tennis?
6 I _____ the day with breakfast.
8 I don't drive to work – I _____.
9 It is only 2p.m. Don't _____ work!

**Down**

1 How do you _____ to work?
5 We _____ in London at three o'clock.
7 Shh! Don't _____ – I'm on the phone!
8 I'm not ready. Please _____ for me.

**B** ▶ 7.2 Listen to the verbs in Exercise 1A and write:

1 one action with the sound in *who* and *room*
   *move* _____

2 two actions with the sound in *cake* and *day*
   _____

3 two actions with the sound in *four* and *door*
   _____

4 two actions with the sound in *like* and *I*
   _____

5 one action with the sound in *car* and *father*
   _____

6 one action with the sound in *have* and *happy*
   _____

7 one action with the sound in *shop* and *coffee*
   _____

# LISTENING

**2 A** Complete the quiz.

## Amazing Animal Facts

Animals are amazing! They walk for days, find the way home and some even speak!

1 **Every winter, an Emperor penguin walks:**
   a) 10–20 kilometres
   b) 30–60 kilometres
   c) 50–120 kilometres

2 **A black and white cat named Tom was lost and travelled in a plane for:**
   a) two weeks
   b) two months
   c) two years

3 **Another amazing cat named Tom walked:**
   a) 4,000 kilometres
   b) 5,000 kilometres
   c) 6,000 kilometres

4 **In its lifetime, a cow gives _____ glasses of milk.**
   a) 50,000    b) 100,000    c) 200,000

5 **Talking parrots know about ten to twenty words, but one famous African grey parrot, N'kisi, used:**
   a) 150 words    b) 450 words    c) 950 words

**B** ▶ 7.3 Listen and check.

**C** Listen again and match 1–5 with a)–e).

1 Emperor penguins
2 Tom the cat (UK)
3 Tom the cat (USA)
4 Cows
5 N'kisi the parrot

a) sometimes live 25 years.
b) was in a test in 2004.
c) travelled 800,000 kilometres.
d) are very big.
e) travelled for two years.

# GRAMMAR
## PAST SIMPLE: REGULAR VERBS

**3 A** Complete the story of Jean. Use the past simple form of the verbs in the box.

> ~~stop~~   arrive   live   want (x2)   like   wait   visit
> stay   walk   help   talk

In 2000, Jean Beliveau was 45 years old. He had a lot of problems with his job, so he ¹ _stopped_ work. He ² _____ to go on a journey, but not with a bus or a train. He ³ _____ to walk. Jean ⁴ _____ in Montreal, Canada, so he ⁵ _____ from Montreal to Atlanta in the USA. He was very happy when he ⁶ _____. He ⁷ _____ walking, so he continued.

Jean ⁸ _____ 64 countries in 11 years. He ⁹ _____ to different people in every country and he often¹⁰ _____ in their homes. Sometimes he was tired, but he didn't stop. Jean's wife ¹¹ _____ for him. She ¹² _____ him on his journey with money and messages. Jean walked around the world. When he arrived home in 2011 he was 56 years old. His family was very happy to see him again.

**B** Correct the information.

1 Jean Beliveau started work in 2000.
   *He didn't start work in 2000. He stopped work.*

2 Jean wanted to stay at home.
   _____

3 Jean travelled by bus.
   _____

4 Jean lived in Atlanta in the USA.
   _____

5 He worked in people's homes.
   _____

6 Jean's wife hated him.
   _____

**4 A** Write the past forms of the verbs.

1 live        _lived_
2 close       _____
3 open        _____
4 listen      _____
5 look        _____
6 study       _____
7 email       _____
8 text        _____
9 stop        _____
10 answer     _____

**B** ▶ 7.4 Listen and write the past forms from Exercise 4A in the correct group.

| /t/ danced |
| --- |
|  |

| /d/ moved |
| --- |
| lived |

| /ɪd/ started |
| --- |
|  |

**C** Add the verbs to the table in Exercise 4B.

1 worked
2 wanted
3 asked
4 played
5 repeated
6 watched

**D** ▶ 7.5 Listen and check. Then listen and repeat.

# VOCABULARY

## ADJECTIVES

**1 A** Put the letters in the correct order to make adjectives. The first letter is underlined.

1 tin<u>i</u>ergents _____interesting_____
2 <u>a</u>terg _____
3 b<u>r</u>reelit _____
4 w<u>a</u>flu _____
5 on<u>b</u>rig _____
6 oili<u>c</u>edus _____
7 atti<u>cf</u>ans _____
8 <u>b</u>da <u>n</u>to _____
9 lal gi<u>r</u>th _____
10 to<u>n</u> yr<u>v</u>e dogo _____

**B** Read the reviews and write hotel (H), film (F), restaurant (R) or concert (C).

**R E V I E W S**

**1** _____
D_____ food and
f_____ waiters!
The best Japanese in town.

**2** _____
The guitar player is n_____
v_____ g_____,
but their music is i_____.

**3** _____
The first ten minutes is
g_____, but then it's really
b_____ for ninety minutes.
The acting is t_____.

**4** _____
The rooms are n_____
b_____ and the breakfast
was a_____ r_____,
but it's on a noisy street. An
a_____ place to sleep.

**C** Cover the words in Exercise 1A. Complete the reviews with the correct adjectives.

# FUNCTION

## ASKING FOR AND GIVING OPINIONS

**2** Put the words in the box in the correct places in the conversation.

| 's wasn't was Was concert 're It awful good |
| --- |

**A:** Hello, Helene. How ⟨'s⟩ the party?

**B:** It's not very.

**A:** Why not?

**B:** There's no music and no food. It's!

**A:** Who's there?

**B:** Well, three people – all students. They boring. Where are you?

**A:** I'm at home, but I was at a rock.

**B:** How it?

**A:** was interesting.

**B:** Interesting? it good?

**A:** Well, no – it very good.

# LEARN TO

## SHOW FEELINGS

**3 A** ▶ 7.6 Listen to the conversations and circle the correct adjectives.

1 interesting/(delicious)  4 not very good/all right
2 terrible/fantastic  5 delicious/awful
3 great/not bad

**B** ▶ 7.7 Listen and check. Then listen and repeat.

## GRAMMAR

### PAST SIMPLE: IRREGULAR VERBS

**1** Complete the sentences with the past simple of the verbs in the box.

| meet | go | break | knows | sit | say | see | take |

**1** They _____met_____ in Paris.

**2** They _____ in a café.

**3** They _____ on a boat.

**4** They _____ Notre Dame.

**5** He _____ her hand.

**6** She _____ 'Goodbye'.

**7** He _____ it was finished.

**8** She _____ his heart.

**2** Write negative sentences. Use the words in brackets.

**1** She said 'Thirty'. (✗ 'Thirteen')
*She didn't say 'Thirteen'.*

**2** He went to the swimming pool. (✗ gym)

_____

**3** We met in Japan. (✗ China)

_____

**4** I knew her sister. (✗ brother)

_____

**5** The taxi took James to the airport. (✗ station)

_____

**3** Complete the sentences with the correct past simple form of the verbs in brackets.

## Why did you leave your partner?

**1** He ____drove____ a Porsche. I ____didn't drive____. (drive)

**2** She _____ a rich and famous actor. I was an actor, but I _____ famous. Or rich. (become)

**3** I _____ home every day at six and cooked dinner. Sometimes he _____ home. (come)

**4** I _____ a lot of friends. He _____ any friends. (have)

**5** He _____ hip-hop was good music. I _____ it was music. (think)

**6** I _____ her nice things on her birthday. She _____ me any presents on my birthday. (give)

## LISTENING

4 A ▷ 8.1 Listen to Jocelyn and Andreas. What is the same about them?

B Complete the table. Then listen again and check.

| Who ... | Jocelyn | Clare | Andreas | Raji |
|---|---|---|---|---|
| 1 studied together? | ✓ | ✓ | | |
| 2 wasn't very good at Italian? | | | | |
| 3 didn't have any friends in Canberra? | | | | |
| 4 loved Indian food? | | | | |
| 5 met on the internet? | | | | |
| 6 talked on the bus? | | | | |
| 7 moved from Sydney? | | | | |
| 8 wrote an email to the other person? | | | | |

## VOCABULARY

### PREPOSITIONS OF PLACE

5 A Complete the text with *in*, *on* or *at*.

# Top tips
## - Where to meet new friends

**Bored with your friends? Or maybe you don't have any friends? Do you want to meet a new friend? These are the top places to go.**

Go to a party. A lot of people ¹ _____at_____ a party want to meet you!

Travel to a new place for a week or two. People are happy ² _____ holiday.

Go to a gym. It's easy to talk to people ³ _____ a gym.

Use a friend-finder website ⁴ _____ the internet.

Take a class – language, yoga, anything. It's easy to meet new people ⁵ _____ a class because you all like the same thing.

Go to big supermarkets. Talk to people ⁶ _____ the supermarket when you wait.

When you travel, talk to people ⁷ _____ the plane or train.

Go out! It's very difficult to meet new people ⁸ _____ home!

B Read the text again. Tick (✓) the ideas you think are good.

6 Complete the conversations using the prompts.

1 **A:** I phoned you last night. Where were you?
   **B:** I / be / not / home. I / be / work
   *I wasn't at home. I was at work.*

2 **A:** Where's your daughter now?
   **B:** She / be / university / Shanghai
   _____
   _____

3 **A:** Hi, Conrad. Where are you?
   **B:** I / be / a taxi / the city centre
   _____
   _____

4 **A:** How do you know about it?
   **B:** We / see / it / television / last night
   _____
   _____

5 **A:** Where are my keys?
   **B:** They / be / the table
   _____
   _____

6 **A:** Were you on your motorbike?
   **B:** No, / I / be / my car
   _____
   _____

## VOCABULARY

### HOLIDAY ACTIVITIES

**1** Complete the puzzle. Look at the clues and fill in the missing verbs about holiday activities.

Look at the grey boxes. What do people always have in their bags on holiday?

1 _____ at a restaurant
2 _____ a good time
3 _____ ill
4 _____ the local water
5 _____ English
6 _____ the local people
7 _____ camping
8 _____ old buildings

## READING

**2 A** Match problems a)–d) with forum entries 1–3. There is one extra problem.

a) Bad weather _____
b) No rooms _____
c) Too expensive _____
d) Health problems _____

## Tell us about:

# Your best bad holiday

**A bad holiday is always terrible …
or is it? Tell us about your best bad holiday.**

**1** In 2009 we went to Portugal. When we arrived, our beach hotel was full, so they gave us a room in the town, two kilometres from the beach. We weren't happy. Then we met some local people. They asked us to their house and we had some real local food, and we danced. It was a real holiday, not a tourist holiday.

*Mark and Sandy T*

**2** My wife and I went to Mexico last year and on the last day we were very ill. We went to hospital, and we were there for two weeks. The doctors were lovely, and we met some really nice people. That was a very interesting time, because we weren't tourists. We 'lived' in Mexico.

*Sven L*

**3** My brothers and sisters live all around the world, and in 2007 we had a big family party at a hotel on a beach in Malaysia. It was in June, and June is usually hot, but that year it rained every day. So we sat in the hotel and read books, played games and talked. We had a really good time, and it was fantastic for our family.

*Lucia D*

**B** Read the text again. Are the sentences true (T) or false (F)?

1 Mark and Sandy stayed on the beach. _____F_____
2 They went to a Portuguese home. _____
3 They ate Portuguese food. _____
4 Sven was in hospital all of his holiday. _____
5 He was bored in hospital. _____
6 His wife was ill, too. _____
7 Lucia's family live in different countries. _____
8 The weather was good. _____
9 They stayed in a flat on the beach. _____
10 They saw a lot of places in Malaysia. _____

# GRAMMAR

## PAST SIMPLE: QUESTIONS

**3 A** Write the questions. Use the verbs in bold.

1 A: *Where did you go* on holiday last summer?
   B: We **went** to Japan.

2 A: _____?
   B: We **went** in August.

3 A: _____ with?
   B: I **travelled** with my friend Ramon.

4 A: _____?
   B: We **saw** Mount Fuji and Kyoto, the old capital.

5 A: _____?
   B: We **ate** a lot of interesting food.

6 A: _____?
   B: We **drank** tea. A lot of tea!

**B** Write past simple questions using the prompts.

1 it / be / your first time / Japan?
   *Was it your first time in Japan?*

2 you / go / Hiroshima?
   _____

3 you / meet / local people?
   _____

4 you / speak / Japanese?
   _____

5 you / have / good time?
   _____

6 be / weather / good?
   _____

**C** Match answers a)–f) with questions 1–6 in Exercise 3B.

a) Yes, *I did*. The best time of my life.          *5*

b) No, _____. It's very difficult, and I didn't study it!          _____

c) Yes, _____. It was hot and sunny.          _____

d) No, _____. I was there in 2004.          _____

e) Yes, _____. They were very friendly.          _____

f) No, _____. There wasn't time.          _____

**D** Complete the short answers above.

# WRITING

## SO AND BECAUSE

**4** Join the sentences using the linkers in brackets.

1 We drank the local water. We were ill. (because)
   *We were ill because we drank the local water.*

2 The restaurants were expensive. I cooked every evening. (so)
   _____

3 I spoke English with the local people. I don't speak French. (because)
   _____

4 We went to bed very late. There was a party in the hotel. (so)
   _____

5 It snowed at night. The train was late. (because)
   _____

6 We went camping. The hotels were all full. (so)
   _____

7 We took a taxi. People said the underground was dangerous. (because)
   _____

8 I don't like hot weather. We went there in April. (so)
   _____

**5** Add *so* or *because* to the sentences.

                    *because*
1 We stayed at home ⋋ it rained all day.

2 I was hungry I ate dinner early.

3 Jason didn't go to the concert he didn't have a ticket.

4 They sat down they were tired.

5 The shops were two kilometres from the house we drove there.

6 The film was awful Yvette and I left after ten minutes.

# VOCABULARY

## PREPOSITIONS OF PLACE

**1** Look at the picture and the clues. Complete the crossword.

Across:
```
    [1]
     
     
     
[2]N  E  A  R
              [3]
              
        [4]
        
[5]          
        
   [6]          
        
      [7]          
           
```

**Across**

2 The mouse is _____ the cheese.
5 The bag is _____ of the carrots.
6 The cat is _____ the mouse.
7 The apples are _____ the fish.

**Down**

1 The cheese is _____ of the cat.
2 The mouse is _____ the tomatoes.
3 The grapes are _____ of the cheese.
4 The fish is _____ the apples and the cheese.

# FUNCTION

## GIVING DIRECTIONS

**2 A** Cross out six extra words in the conversation.

**A:** Excuse ~~for~~ me, where's the ticket office?
**B:** It's between of the trains and the buses.
**A:** OK. Thanks. And where are at the payphones?
**B:** Do you see the café over on there?
**A:** Yes, I do see.
**B:** They're behind of the café.

**B** Read the conversation again. Where are the ticket office and payphones in the picture?

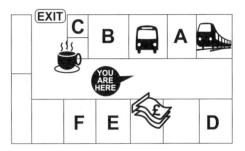

**C** ▶ 8.2 Listen to the conversations. Match places 1–4 with A–F in the picture.

1 underground _____    3 women's toilets _____
2 men's toilets _____    4 taxis _____

# LEARN TO

## USE EXAMPLES

**3 A** Complete the conversations with the words in the box.

~~job~~   adjective   know   fruit   example

**Conversation 1**

**A:** Oh, you're a teacher. And what's your husband's
¹ _____job_____?
**B:** What's that?
**A:** You ² _____ – doctor, teacher, secretary.
**B:** Oh, he's a pilot.

**Conversation 2**

**A:** What ³ _____ do they have in the supermarket today?
**B:** I don't understand.
**A:** Like, do they have apples, bananas, oranges?
**B:** Oh, OK. They have apples and oranges.

**Conversation 3**

**A:** Do you know another ⁴ _____ for 'good'?
**B:** Another what?
**A:** For ⁵ _____, good, bad, hot, cold, happy …
**B:** Oh, I understand. I know another word for 'very good'. Fantastic!

**B** ▶ 8.3 Listen and check. Then listen again and say A's part with the speaker.

**GRAMMAR** PAST SIMPLE

**1 A** Complete the text with the past simple of the verbs in brackets.

# On holiday in the 1960s

Our family holiday ¹____was____ (be) always the same. We ² _____ (not go) by plane and we ³ _____ (not stay) in a hotel – planes and hotels ⁴ _____ (be) too expensive. We ⁵ _____ (travel) by car and we always ⁶ _____ (go) camping near the sea. The roads ⁷ _____ (not be) bad and we ⁸ _____ (drive) about 600 kilometres at night. We usually ⁹ _____ (arrive) at the campsite at about 7a.m. and we ¹⁰_____ (have) breakfast next to the car, on the ground. Our holiday always ¹¹_____ (start) with this breakfast together, then we ¹² _____ (walk) along the beach and ¹³ _____ (go) to bed – at 11 o'clock in the morning! I really ¹⁴ _____ (love) those holidays.

**B** Complete the questions with the correct form of the verbs in the box.

| ~~drive~~   have (x2)   be   stay   go |
| --- |

1 _Did you drive_ _____ at night?
2 _____ in a hotel?
3 _____ breakfast in the car?
4 _____ tired when you arrived?
5 _____ swimming in the sea?
6 _____ a good time?

**C** Match answers a)–f) with questions 1–6 in Exercise 1B.

a) No, _____, not on the first morning. We walk on the beach. ____5____
b) Yes, _____, so we went to bed. _____
c) No, _____. We ate next to it. _____
d) Yes, _____. A wonderful time. _____
e) Yes, _____. We left in the evening and arrived in the morning. _____
f) No, _____. It was too expensive. _____

**D** Complete the short answers in Exercise 1C.

**2 A** Read the messages in Bob's blog. Then put the words in the correct order to make questions.

> 27th July: back from a week in Thailand. Fantastic holiday, beautiful weather, lovely people.
>
> Nina and the children loved it. A lot of time on the beach – the children played, we did a lot of reading. The only problem was the journey home. There were problems with the plane – we waited four hours at the airport, so we only got home at twelve o'clock last night!

1 Bob / holiday? / Where / on / did / go
   _Where did Bob go on holiday?_
2 he / did / travel? / How
   _____
3 go? / did / When / he
   _____
4 with? / Who / he / did / go
   _____
5 holiday? / they / did / What / do / on
   _____
6 home / late? / Why / they / were
   _____

**B** Answer the questions in Exercise 2A.

1 _He went to Thailand._
2 _____
3 _____
4 _____
5 _____
6 _____

**3 A** Write the past tense of the verbs.

| 1 | like | _liked_ | 9 | become | _____ |
|---|------|---------|----|--------|----------|
| 2 | start | _____ | 10 | say | _____ |
| 3 | speak | _____ | 11 | take | _____ |
| 4 | know | _____ | 12 | think | _____ |
| 5 | cry | _____ | 13 | stop | _____ |
| 6 | look | _____ | 14 | listen | _____ |
| 7 | want | _____ | 15 | study | _____ |
| 8 | talk | _____ | 16 | meet | _____ |

**B** ▶ R4.1 Listen and check.

**C** Listen again and underline the main stress in the past forms in Exercise 3A.

_liked_

_started_

## VOCABULARY REVIEW 1

**4** Find four words for each group 1–5.

| S | E | E | O | L | D | B | U | I | L | D | I | N | G | S |
|---|---|---|---|---|---|---|---|---|---|---|---|---|---|---|
| Y | J | Y | N | O | V | E | M | B | E | R | L | D | A | B |
| N | F | W | G | E | F | B | O | P | P | O | S | I | T | E |
| X | A | A | A | G | B | A | K | H | G | Z | B | X | E | T |
| B | N | L | P | O | Z | T | P | Q | G | I | R | C | R | W |
| E | T | K | A | C | Y | U | H | Q | X | A | R | X | R | E |
| H | A | V | E | A | G | O | O | D | T | I | M | E | I | E |
| I | S | Z | Q | M | Y | L | P | X | E | L | J | A | B | N |
| N | T | R | G | P | L | A | Y | T | R | A | V | E | L | Q |
| D | I | R | W | I | B | T | G | N | E | A | R | M | E | B |
| L | C | J | A | N | U | A | R | Y | A | W | F | U | L | O |
| K | J | A | B | G | G | S | E | P | T | E | M | B | E | R |
| P | K | B | M | W | H | K | J | U | N | E | N | P | I | I |
| S | P | E | A | K | E | N | G | L | I | S | H | C | F | N |
| Z | R | K | B | X | Y | A | L | T | R | Y | F | A | Z | G |

**1** Holiday activities
*see old buildings*

**2** Actions

**3** Months

**4** Prepositions of place

**5** Adjectives

## VOCABULARY REVIEW 2

**5** Read the sentences and complete sentence **6** with the correct name.

**1** Bob's house is opposite Alan's house.
**2** Chuck's house is on the right of Bob's house.
**3** Chuck's house is between Bob and Dale's house.
**4** Dale's house is in front of Frank's house.
**5** My car is on the left of Frank's house.
**6** My car is behind _____'s house.

## FUNCTION REVISION

**6 A** Underline the correct alternatives in the conversations.

**Conversation 1**
**A:** ¹*Is there/Is it* a good restaurant near here?
**B:** ²*There's/Is* a good Chinese restaurant over there.
**A:** Where?
**B:** ³*On the left/Opposite* of the bank.
**A:** I see it. Is the food good?
**B:** Well, I think it's ⁴*delicious/awful.*

**Conversation 2**
**A:** Do you know the Chinese restaurant ⁵*near/in front* here?
**C:** Yes.
**A:** Is it good?
**C:** It's ⁶*right/all right*, but I like Italian food. ⁷*There's/There are* a great Italian restaurant ⁸*opposite/on right of* the school.
**A:** Where?
**C:** ⁹*Behind/Between* the bus over there. ¹⁰*Next to/Next* the newsagent's.
**A:** Oh, right. Yes. ¹¹*How's/Who's* the food there?
**C:** We ate there last night. It was ¹²*boring/fantastic.*

**B** ▷ R4.2 Listen and check.

## CHECK

Circle the correct option to complete the sentences.

**1** Excuse me, _____ a supermarket near here?
   a) is there
   b) here is
   c) is where

**2** Ralph _____ here yesterday.
   a) wasn't
   b) weren't
   c) no was

**3** He _____ home last week.
   a) tried
   b) waited
   c) moved

**4** A: Were you at work?
   B: Yes, _____.
   a) was I
   b) I was
   c) you were

**5** I _____ your friend.
   a) didn't met
   b) didn't meet
   c) wasn't meet

**6** We watched, but we _____.
   a) didn't played
   b) not played
   c) didn't play

**7** A: Where's the football?
   B: It's _____ the tree.
   a) behind of
   b) behind
   c) on the right

**8** He _____ the door with his key.
   a) was open
   b) open
   c) opened

**9** March, April, _____
   a) June
   b) May
   c) July

**10** _____ the bank over there?
   a) There you see
   b) Do you see
   c) Let me check

**11** A: That was fantastic!
   B: Yes, it was _____!
   a) delicious
   b) terrible
   c) boring

**12** He's _____ home.
   a) in
   b) on
   c) at

**13** Today's the _____ of September.
   a) fiveteenth
   b) fifteenth
   c) fivteenth

**14** A: How's the book?
   B: _____ very good.
   a) I think it's
   b) I think is
   c) I think it

**15** _____ Spanish?
   a) Did you speak
   b) Did you spoke
   c) Spoke you

**16** The film was _____.
   a) all right
   b) delicious
   c) very not good

**17** A: Did you see us?
   B: No, I _____.
   a) didn't see
   b) didn't
   c) don't saw

**18** Peru was great! We _____ a really good time!
   a) had
   b) were
   c) got

**19** We _____ for our holiday.
   a) did camping
   b) went camp
   c) went camping

**20** He _____ home last week.
   a) go
   b) wents
   c) went

RESULT     /20

# 9)) SHOPPING

## VOCABULARY

### MONEY

**1 A** Circle six money verbs and their past tense forms.

| | | | | | | |
|---|---|---|---|---|---|---|
| P | A | I | D | C | O | S | T |
| A | E | G | O | T | K | K | D |
| Y | A | C | D | G | A | V | E |
| S | B | O | U | G | H | T | N |
| G | F | S | S | R | N | G | M |
| Q | S | T | H | B | H | I | J |
| E | E | I | B | F | G | V | O |
| L | L | P | U | S | G | E | T |
| Q | L | R | Y | S | O | L | D |

**B** Complete the conversation with the words in Exercise 1A.

**A:** Where did you ¹ _____buy_____ that smartphone?

**B:** I ² _____ it online.

**A:** How much did it ³ _____?

**B:** It ⁴ _____ eighty euros.

**A:** Really? I ⁵ _____ sixty euros for the same one last year.

**B:** Did I ⁶ _____ too much?

**A:** I don't know. Maybe.

**B:** And where's your smartphone now?

**A:** It wasn't right, so I ⁷ _____ it online.

**B:** Why did you ⁸ _____ it?

**A:** It was a birthday present for my son Andy, but it was too big.

**B:** So your son doesn't have a smartphone now.

**A:** Yes, he does. He ⁹ _____ one from his grandfather!

**B:** And what did Andy ¹⁰ _____ from you?

**A:** What did I ¹¹ _____ Andy? I ¹² _____ him the money!

## READING

**2 A** Look at the pictures. Which ones do you think are good gifts for women (✓) and which ones are bad? (✗)

**B** Read the article and check your ideas.

### SIX GIFTS <u>NOT</u> TO GIVE YOUR WIFE OR GIRLFRIEND

Sometimes it's difficult to buy a good gift, and easy to buy a bad one. Next time you shop for a present for your girlfriend or wife, take this list ... and **DON'T** buy these things!

- **Clothes** – they're always the wrong size, the wrong colour or just wrong.

- **A gift certificate to a gym** – this gift tells her 'You're too fat!'

- A cookbook – the message here is 'You're a bad cook' or 'Please cook for me.'

- **A photo frame with no picture** – a frame with no picture is a big question mark. Put a picture of the two of you in the frame (and NOT a picture of you alone!).

- **A set of luggage** – maybe she needs luggage, but from you this gift says 'I want you to leave me.'

- **A vase with no flowers** – this is the same as a photo frame with no picture. It's an empty feeling. Give her flowers, but no vase. Yes, flowers die, but true love never dies!

**C** Read the women's sentences. Which gift did they get?

**1** 'But I make dinner for you every night!' _____a cookbook_____

**2** 'They're very useful ... but do you think I need a holiday?' _____

**3** 'You bought me the same gift last year and I only went three times!' _____

**4** 'They're fantastic. Really beautiful!' _____

**5** 'It's nice, but where am I?' _____

**6** 'I like it. Let me get something from the garden to put in it.' _____

**7** 'It's red. You know I don't like red!' _____

## GRAMMAR

### OBJECT PRONOUNS

**3 A** Complete the table.

| Subject pronoun | Object pronoun |
|---|---|
| I | 1 _____ me |
| 2 _____ | you |
| he | 3 _____ |
| 4 _____ | her |
| it | 5 _____ |
| 6 _____ | us |
| they | 7 _____ |

**B** Complete the text with object pronouns (*me*, *you*, etc.).

I'm not a bad person. But I'm not very lucky with gift-giving. I bought my husband a beautiful, expensive pen, but he had two of $^1$ _them_. When I gave $^2$ _____ the pen box, he opened $^3$ _____ and said, 'Great – number three!' I got a clock for my mother, and she hated $^4$ _____.
'Clocks are for old people, not for $^5$ _____', she said. 'I'm not old!' I found a lovely scarf for my sister. I sent $^6$ _____ to $^7$ _____ in the post but she never got $^8$ _____. Then my birthday came, and my husband, mother and sister gave $^9$ _____ a box. 'This is for $^{10}$ _____!' they said. 'Happy Birthday from all of $^{11}$ _____!' I opened $^{12}$ _____. Inside was a pen, a clock and a scarf. I laughed with all of $^{13}$ _____.

**4** Look at the conversations. Complete B's part with the correct pronoun. Use the words in bold to help.

**1 A:** Are **Denny** and **Barb** at home?
**B:** I don't know. I phoned _them_, but _they_ didn't answer.

**2 A:** When did you see **Anna**?
**B:** _____ was at the office. I gave _____ your number.

**3 A:** So, how's the **new flat**?
**B:** I like _____ a lot. _____'s small, but _____'s good for me.

**4 A:** Hey, how does Martin know **you two**?
**B:** _____ met him at a party. He told _____ about you.

**5 A:** I didn't get **your emails**.
**B:** Sorry, maybe I sent _____ to the wrong address. _____ weren't important.

**6 A:** Hello, nice to meet you. **I'm** Sue.
**B:** _____ think _____ know you from somewhere. Do you remember _____? My name's Gill.

## WRITING

### LISTINGS

**5 A** Read the text and match listings 1–4 with items A–D.

# Free to a good home ...

**1 Bedroom clock**

Would you like a free clock? Someone gave it to my mother. The clock is my mother's clock. The clock is white and quite big. My mother says the clock is new. She likes the clock, but she doesn't use the clock.

**2 Music!**

My best friends Tim and Carla write and play music. Tim and Carla are very good and Tim and Carla's new music is great. Tim and Carla want to practise the new music. Tim and Carla play Friday and Saturday evenings. Phone and talk to Tim and Carla about times and dates.

**3 Car radio**

Does anyone want a car radio? The car radio is from my brother's car, but my brother's car doesn't work, so my brother doesn't want the radio. The car radio works well, but my brother and I don't need the car radio.

**4 Dolce and Gabbana jeans**

I bought some Dolce and Gabbana jeans last year. The jeans are size 8 and very nice, but the jeans are too small for me now, and I don't want the jeans.

**B** Rewrite the underlined parts of the listings using pronouns (*it, she, he, we, they, them, him*) or possessive adjectives (*his, her, their*).

~~The clock~~ *It* is ~~my mother's~~ *her* clock

# GRAMMAR

## LIKE, LOVE, HATE + -ING

**1** Look at the table and write sentences about Kate and Theo.

| | Kate | Theo |
|---|---|---|
| 1 | ✗ | ✓✓ |
| 2 | ✓ | ✗✗ |
| 3 | ✗✗ | ✓ |
| 4 | ✓✓ | ✗ |
| 5 | ✓ | ✓✓ |

| love | like | don't like | hate |
|---|---|---|---|
| ✓✓ | ✓ | ✗ | ✗✗ |

1 *Kate doesn't like playing tennis. Theo loves playing tennis.*

2 _____

_____

3 _____

_____

4 _____

_____

5 _____

_____

**2** Complete the sentences with the *-ing* form of the verbs in the box.

go   lose   eat   drink   arrive
get up   dance   walk

What do you hate? I hate …

1 ___*going*___ camping in winter. It's too cold!
2 _____ bad coffee. I love coffee, and bad coffee is a waste of money.
3 _____ in a restaurant alone. Everybody looks at me!
4 _____ to bad music. I feel so stupid.
5 _____ early. My best rest time is morning.
6 _____ in the rain with my girlfriend. Or alone. It's not romantic!
7 _____ the key to my flat. I only have one key!
8 _____ late for a film. It's important to see the beginning!

**3 A** Write the *-ing* form of the verbs.

| | | | | | |
|---|---|---|---|---|---|
| 1 | break | _____ | 7 | move | _____ |
| 2 | come | _____ | 8 | stay | _____ |
| 3 | cry | _____ | 9 | see | _____ |
| 4 | laugh | _____ | 10 | talk | _____ |
| 5 | leave | _____ | 11 | wait | _____ |
| 6 | make | _____ | 12 | watch | _____ |

**B** Underline the correct alternatives.

**1**

**A:** We saw *Jurassic World* online yesterday.
**B:** I don't like [1]*watching/waiting* films online.
**A:** I [2]*love/don't like* going to the cinema – it's too crowded and noisy.

**2**

**A:** Do you like [3]*making/moving* cakes?
**B:** Yes, I [4]*like/do*. It's relaxing. What about you?
**A:** Me? No, I [5]*hate/don't* it. I never cook.

**3**

**A:** Do you [6]*like/talk* parties?
**B:** No, I [7]*don't/don't like*. I usually leave early. And you?
**A:** I love parties. I really like [8]*talking/laughing* to new people.

**4**

**A:** What [9]*are/do* you like doing on holiday?
**B:** I love going to old cities and [10]*staying/seeing* old buildings.

## VOCABULARY

### ACTIVITIES

4 Look at the pictures and write the activities.

1 t*aking p*hotos

2 s_____

3 r_____

4 c_____

5 g_____ to the
t_____

6 r_____

7 ch_____
o_____

8 p_____
c_____
g_____

9 g_____
for l_____
w_____

10 c_____

## LISTENING

5 A ▶ 9.1 Listen and match the speakers with the activity gifts. There is one gift you don't need.

Speaker 1 _____
Speaker 2 _____
Speaker 3 _____
Speaker 4 _____

A **hot-air balloon trip**

B *camping holiday*

C **salsa lessons**

D **Driving a Formula-1 car**

E **bird-watching day**

B Listen again and complete the table.

| Speaker | liked it (✓) / didn't like it (✗) | because |
|---|---|---|
| 1 | ✓ | • He liked the music.<br>• Cheryl was a great dancer.<br>• They laughed. |
| 2 | | •<br>• |
| 3 | | • |
| 4 | | •<br>•<br>• |

## VOCABULARY
### SHOPPING DEPARTMENTS

1 Read Pete's shopping list and complete the crossword with department names.

Crossword:
1 across: JEWELLERY
4 down: L
5 down: C
6 down: C
7 down: D
8 across: C
9 across: T
10 across: W
11 across: S

### shopping list

1 a ring (_____ & Watches)
2 a TV (Home _____)
3 a bag (Travel & _____)
4 a lamp for the office (Furniture & _____)
5 shoes for me (Men's _____ and Shoes)
6 school shoes for Emily (_____ clothes & Shoes)
7 a bottle of water (Food & _____)
8 a mouse (_____ & Phones)
9 a game for Billy and Emily (_____)
10 a sweater for Sue (_____ clothes & Shoes)
11 a football for Billy (_____)

PETE    BILLY    EMILY    SUE

## FUNCTION
### MAKING REQUESTS

2 A ▶ 9.2 Listen and match conversations 1–3 with places a)–c).
a) someone's home _____
b) a shop _____
c) café _____

B Put the words in the box in the correct place to complete the conversations.

like (x2)   a   ~~you~~   that   'd   I'd   I

**Conversation 1**
A: What would ⋀ like? *(you)*
B: I like a cheese sandwich.
A: Would you white bread or brown?
B: Brown, please.

**Conversation 2**
A: Can help you?
B: Yes, I'd that sweater, please.
A: This one?
B: No. I'd like brown one, please.

**Conversation 3**
A: Come in. Sit down.
B: Nice flat!
A: Thanks. Would you like drink?
B: Yes, love an apple juice or something.

C Listen again and check.

## LEARN TO
### USE HESITATION PHRASES

3 A ▶ 9.3 Listen to the questions and write your answers.
1 _____
2 _____
3 _____
4 _____

B ▶ 9.4 Listen to someone answer the questions. Which question does she not answer?

C Listen again and number the hesitation phrases in the order you hear them.
a) Let me think. ___1___
b) Well … _____
c) Um … _____
d) Er … _____
e) Oh, I don't know. _____
f) Let me see … _____

4 A Write hesitation phrases at the beginning of your answers in Exercise 3A.

B ▶ 9.3 Listen again to the questions and practise answering with the hesitation phrases.

## VOCABULARY
### COLLOCATIONS

**1** Cross out the incorrect alternative.

1 coffee — make — clothes / ~~golf~~

2 German — speak — England / three languages

3 a computer — use — a knife and fork / a piano

4 a seat — read — a map / a newspaper

5 a name — remember — information / golf

6 bean — cook — lunch / Chinese food

7 a plane — ride — a horse / a bike

8 football — play — words / tennis

## LISTENING

**2 A** Match jobs 1–5 with problems a)–e).

1 shop assistant ___c___
2 tour guide _____
3 chef _____
4 hairdresser _____
5 waiter _____

a) You can't remember the drinks people want.
b) The customer says, 'It's too short.'
c) You don't know any prices.
d) You don't like food.
e) People can't understand your English.

**B** ▶ 10.1 Listen to people talk about their new jobs. Write the jobs from Exercise 2A.

Speaker 1 _____
Speaker 2 _____
Speaker 3 _____

**C** Listen again and write the number of the speaker.

Who:
1 didn't know answers to questions? ___1___
2 laughed at a customer? _____
3 spoke another language very well? _____
4 had a bad second day? _____
5 thought he/she lost the job? _____
6 had the wrong information? _____

## GRAMMAR
### CAN/CAN'T

**3** **A** Look at the pictures and write the sentences.

**1** *He can't remember names, but he can remember numbers.*

**2** She _____ .

**3** He _____ .

**4** She _____ .

**5** He _____ .

**6** She _____ .

**B** ▶ 10.2 Listen and check. Then listen and say the sentences with the recording. Pay attention to the pronunciation of *can* /kən/ and *can't* /kɑːnt/.

**4** Put the words in bold in the correct order in the conversations.

**Conversation 1**

**A:** Hi, Stefanie. [1]**you / Can / me? / help**
    *Can you help me?*

**B:** Yes, is there a problem?

**A:** Yes, [2]**read / you / the / address / email / can** on this business card?

_____

**B:** Let me look.

**A:** [3]**it / very / can't / I / see / well.** I don't have my glasses.

_____

**B:** It says globaltiger@nortex.com.

**A:** Thanks.

**Conversation 2**

**A:** I studied languages at university.

**B:** [4]**you / speak? / What / can / languages**

_____

**A:** [5]**speak / I / and / can / Russian / Italian.**

_____

**B:** Privyet.*

**A:** Oh, you speak Russian!

**B:** Yes, [6]**very / not / but / well.**

_____

* *Privyet = hello* in Russian.

**Conversation 3**

**A:** Big problem. The chef is ill.

**B:** That's OK. [7]**can / I / cook.**

_____

**A:** But [8]**you / Spanish / can / cook / food?**

_____

**B:** Yes, [9]**it / quite / I / cook / can / well.**

_____

**A:** OK, you have the job!

## VOCABULARY

### LIFE CHANGES

**1 A** Complete the phrases.

1 s*ave*_____ money
2 c_____ jobs
3 h_____ others
4 g_____ fit
5 s_____ smoking
6 l_____ weight
7 w_____ less and relax more
8 l_____ something new
9 s_____ more time with friends and family
10 g_____ organised

**B** Match sentences a)–j) with phrases 1–10 in Exercise 1A.

a) 'It's expensive and it's bad for you!'  ___5___
b) 'Do sport every day.'  _____
c) 'Put your important papers in boxes. Write dates on the boxes.'  _____
d) 'Fifty hours a week is too much!'  _____
e) 'Give money or give your time'  _____
f) 'For example, a language or a hobby'  _____
g) 'Stop eating chocolate!'  _____
h) 'Yes, money is important, but it's important to like your work, too!'  _____
i) 'Put a little in the bank every week.'  _____
j) 'Go to a restaurant together.'  _____

**C** Complete the texts with the past forms of phrases from Exercise 1A.

# Life changes
## ... aren't always good

Last January I was 150 kilograms. I wanted to change, so I ate less and I ¹____*lost*____ a lot of ____*weight*____: 20 kilograms. I went to the gym every day and I ²_____ very _____. But after two months I became bored. Now it's June and I weigh 150 kilograms again!

For ten years I worked in a bank, then last year I ³_____ _____ and became a chef in a French restaurant. But I hate it. It's very hard and I'm always tired!

Last month I moved office. I bought some boxes and put everything in the correct place. I ⁴_____ really _____. My office is beautiful, but now I can't find things. That wasn't a problem before.

Last year I became very tired because I was at work twelve hours a day. So I ⁵_____ less and _____ more. I ⁶_____ more time _____ my friends. But often my friends didn't have a lot of time, and I was bored. So I went back to work!

## READING

**2 A** Read the article and tick (✓) the ideas you think are good.

# How to reach your goals

**Here's a typical situation. Someone says, 'I'm going to lose weight', 'I'm going to change jobs', 'I'm going to stop smoking.' One month, two months or one year later, there's no change. When we have a goal, how can we be sure we reach it? Here are seven top tips:**

**1** Write the goal on a piece of paper. Put it over your desk.

**2** Tell a friend your goal. Ask him or her for help.

**3** Don't talk about it a lot – you lose energy that way. Talking is not doing. You want to <u>do</u>.

**4** Make the goal concrete. Don't say, 'I'm going to save money'; say, 'I'm going to save $1,000 in six months.'

**5** Give a start and finish date.

**6** Be sure the goal is <u>your</u> goal, not a goal that someone gave you.

**7** Do something to reach your goal every day.

**B** Match mistakes a)–f) with ideas 1–7 above.

a) I want to change my job some time in the future.  ___4, 5___
b) Today I didn't do anything about a new job.  _____
c) I talk to everyone about my goal, all the time.  _____
d) I wrote a note on my computer: 'Next year I'm going to change my job.' Now I can't find the note.  _____
e) My best friend said, 'Look for a job with more money,' but money isn't important to me.  _____
f) I don't talk to anyone about my goal.  _____

## GRAMMAR
### BE GOING TO

**3** Complete the sentences with the correct form (positive or negative) of the verbs in brackets.

1 She ___'s going to change___ her name because she doesn't like the name 'Princess'. (change)

2 Good morning. I'm Jack Soames and today I _____ about the problems with city transport. (talk)

3 The weather's bad, so I _____ the mountain today. It's too dangerous. (climb)

4 They _____ to bed early tonight because their bus leaves at six o'clock tomorrow morning. (go)

5 Jaime has problems with his English, so tomorrow his teacher _____ him with extra lessons. (help)

6 Mark and Ruth don't like parties, so they _____ on Friday. (come)

7 My mother can't read maps, so we _____ a GPS for her car. (buy)

8 We _____ to Scotland because there's a very good, fast train service and the roads aren't very good. (drive)

9 There's something wrong with my computer, so Jim _____ at it. (look)

10 Tina really loves her old camera, so she _____ it. (sell)

**4** Put the words in the box in the correct place to complete the conversation.

| to | going | be | not | go | they | isn't | 'm |
|----|-------|-----|-----|-----|------|-------|-----|

**A:** Hi, Sal. Do you have any plans for the weekend?

**B:** We're going ⋀ visit Mario and Julia tonight.
  *to*

**A:** Oh, really? I going to see them tomorrow.

**B:** Yeah, they're only going to here for a week. Then are going to fly back to Saigon.

**A:** I know. I'm going to to Saigon in June.

**B:** Great. So do you want to meet this weekend?

**A:** Well, yeah. I'm going to go for a long walk tomorrow. Do you want to come with me?

**B:** Sure. I'm going to work tomorrow, so let's meet.

**A:** How about Barry?

**B:** He going to come. He's to stay home and study.

**5** Write true sentences using the prompts.

1 I / change jobs / next year
  *I'm going to/I'm not going to change jobs next year.*

2 I / move house / soon
  _____

3 My friends and I / meet / this weekend
  _____

4 My teacher / teach me / next year
  _____

5 I / do sport / this weekend
  _____

6 Liam and Otto / phone me / tonight
  _____

## WRITING
### CHECKING YOUR WORK

**6** Read the email. Find and correct:
  **a)** five mistakes with the punctuation/capital letters
  **b)** five mistakes with the verbs

Hi Elif,

Did you get my email. I was in Istanbul for three days. I wanted to meet, but i didn't got a text or email back from you. I seen Istanbul alone. I go to the Blue Mosque on monday. It was fantastic? On Tuesday I went to the market and bought a jacket a ring and a lamp. It were really interesting. I take a lot of photos.

Jayne

# FUNCTION

## STARTING AND ENDING CONVERSATIONS

**1 A** Cross out the extra word in each sentence.

1 What do you ~~do~~ think of the food?
2 Let's ~~to~~ have a coffee.
3 This is ~~be~~ a great party.
4 So are you from ~~all~~ around here?
5 Oh … is that the late time?
6 Hi, how are you do?
7 I hope we meet us again.
8 I have to a meeting tomorrow at eight o'clock.
9 I can to see an old friend over there.
10 Nice to talk on to you.

**B** Complete the conversations with sentences 1–10 in Exercise 1A.

**Conversation 1**

**A:** ᵃ____*What do you think of the food?*____
**B:** I think it's really good. It's a nice restaurant.
**A:** ᵇ_____
**B:** No, thanks. It's very late.
**A:** ᶜ_____
My train is at eleven o'clock.
**B:** Yes. And ᵈ_____
**A:** Oh! That's early!

**Conversation 2**

**A:** ᵉ_____
**B:** I'm fine, thanks. I'm Katie.
**A:** I'm Sam. ᶠ_____
**B:** Yes, it's really good.
  ᵍ_____
**A:** No, I'm from Sydney in Australia. Er … I'm sorry, ʰ_____
**B:** Oh. Well …
  ⁱ_____
**A:** You too.
  ʲ_____
**B:** Yes. Maybe.

**C** ▶ 10.3 Listen and check.

# LEARN TO

## USE TWO-PART EXCHANGES

**2 A** Match the sentence halves to complete the responses.

a) Yes, it's          1 mine.
b) You             2 so, too.
c) Here's           3 really good.
d) I hope           4 too.

**B** Match the sentences with responses a)–d) in Exercise 2A.

1 I hope you're at the party on Friday.   ____d____
2 This is a nice place.            _____
3 I hope you like the film.          _____
4 This is my email address.         _____
5 I like this restaurant!           _____
6 Here's my card.               _____
7 I hope we meet again.           _____
8 Very nice to meet you.           _____

**C** ▶ 10.4 Listen and check. Then listen and repeat.

# VOCABULARY

## SAYING GOODBYE

**3 A** Find ten words in the wordsnake.

**B** Use the words from the wordsnake to make expressions for saying goodbye. Use some words more than once.

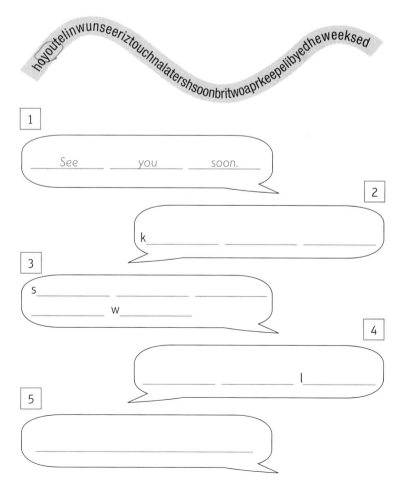

hoyoutelinwunseeriztouchnalatershsoonbritwoaprkeepelibyedheweeksed

1
See  you  soon.

2
ᵏ_____ _____ _____

3
ˢ_____ _____ _____
_____ ʷ_____

4
_____ _____ ˡ_____

5
_____

## GRAMMAR REVISION

**1 A** Complete the texts with a word/phrase from the box. You do not need to use one word/phrase.

**1**

| dancing | can't | like | going to |
| to | going | dance | 's |

My girlfriend Matilda loves ª __dancing__ , and she can ᵇ_____ very well. My problem is that I ᶜ_____ dance, and I don't ᵈ_____ dancing, so I hate ᵉ_____ to parties. Next month we're going ᶠ_____ get married. There ᵍ_____ going to be dancing, and of course the first dance is for me and Matilda. What can I do?

Martin

**2**

| are | can't | going | went | us |
| hated | him | 's going |

Many years ago, my husband Herb and I ª_____ to the sea every summer, but our little son Wally always ᵇ_____ going in the water. So we didn't take ᶜ_____ to the beach. He's fourteen years old now, but he ᵈ_____ swim. Next year Herb and I ᵉ_____ going to go on a beach holiday and we want Wally to come with ᶠ_____. He says he ᵍ_____ to stay at home. What can we do?

Kensie

**3**

| it | can | make | do | are |
| studying | like | going |

I like ª_____ English and I always ᵇ_____ my homework, but I don't often speak in class because I don't ᶜ_____ my pronunciation. I'm ᵈ_____ to change jobs soon and in my new job the meetings ᵉ_____ going to be in English. I ᶠ_____ read and write English, but I can't speak ᵍ_____. What can I do?

Daniel

**B** Write questions using the prompts.

**1** can / Martin / dance?
*Can Martin dance?*

**2** he / like / dance?
_____

**3** can / Matilda / dance?
_____

**4** Matilda / like / dance?
_____

**5** can / Wally / swim?
_____

**6** Wally / like / water?
_____

**7** Daniel / do / his homework?
_____

**8** can / he / read / write English?
_____

**C** Complete the answers to the questions in Exercise 1B.

**1** No, he *can't* .
**2** No, he _____ .
**3** Yes, she _____ .
**4** Yes, she _____ .
**5** No, he _____ .
**6** No, he _____ .
**7** Yes, he _____ .
**8** Yes, he _____ .

**2 A** Read the replies to the problems in 1A. Find and correct two mistakes in each answer.

Dear Martin,

Many people say they can't dancing. Can you walk? Can you jump? Then you can dance. Remember, Matilda loves dancing and she loves you. You going to be fine!

Dear Kensie,

Wally don't can stay home alone, he's 14 and that's very young. He can take swimming lessons? Or can you go on a mountain holiday?

Dear Daniel,

You say you don't often speak in class. But do you sometimes speak? Can people they understand you? Then your pronunciation is not a problem and you can to speak English just fine.

**B** Read the replies again. Which do you think is the best?

## VOCABULARY REVISION

**3** Complete the phrases.

| | |
|---|---|
| **L** | Travel & Lu*ggage*<br>speak two la_____<br>see you la_____<br>work le_____ and relax more |
| **C** | playing co_____ games<br>Children's Cl_____ & Shoes<br>c_____ Japanese food<br>make co_____ |
| **T** | spend more ti_____ with friends and family<br>going to the th_____<br>play te_____<br>keep in to_____ |
| **S** | stop sm_____<br>see you so_____<br>Mens Clothes & Sh_____<br>learn so_____ new |
| **F** **P** **H** | get fi_____<br>cook Italian fo_____<br>take ph_____<br>remember ph_____ numbers |
| **W** | read wo_____ in Arabic<br>lose we_____<br>see you in two we_____<br>go for long wa_____ |
| **O** | help ot_____<br>get or_____<br>chat on_____<br>see an ol_____ friend |

## FUNCTION REVISION

**4 A** Complete the poems.

**1**

**A:** Good morning. ¹___*Would*___ you like a drink?

**B:** It's very hot. Um … I can't think.

**A:** Well, would you ² _____ a cup of tea?

**B:** Nice idea. ³_____ I have three?!

**2**

**A:** Is that the ⁴_____? My train's at three.

**B:** Here's my card. James Bond – that's me.

**A:** Goodbye. I hope we meet ⁵_____.

**B:** Let's meet tonight at half past ten.

**3**

**A:** This is my friend from work, Marty.

**B:** Nice to ⁶_____ you. How's the party?

**C:** The music's bad, I hate this ⁷_____,
But nice to see a friendly face.

**4**

**A:** Sorry, I can see an old friend over ⁸_____,
The woman near the office chair.

**B:** That's not your friend! That's my wife, Flo.

**A:** Well, nice ⁹_____ meet you. Time to go!

**B** ▶ R5.1 Listen and check. Then listen and say the poems with the recording.

## CHECK

Circle the correct option to complete the sentences.

**1** I can speak Japanese, but I _____ write it.
   **a)** can't very well
   **b)** can't
   **c)** don't can

**2 A:** Excuse me. Where are the televisions?
   **B:** They're in Home _____.
   **a)** Entertainment
   **b)** Luggage
   **c)** and Garden

**3** My boyfriend doesn't like _____ to parties.
   **a)** go
   **b)** going
   **c)** goes

**4** So are you _____ here?
   **a)** from around
   **b)** around
   **c)** from this

**5 A:** When can I see _____?
   **B:** I don't know. Phone _____ tomorrow.
   **a)** you, us
   **b)** you, our
   **c)** your, us

**6** _____ you like a drink?
   **a)** Would
   **b)** Do
   **c)** Did

**7** I _____ coffee every morning.
   **a)** cook
   **b)** do
   **c)** make

**8** I _____ get a new job.
   **a)** 'm going to
   **b)** going to
   **c)** 'm going

**9** I _____ tea, please. Thanks.
   **a)** like
   **b)** 'd want
   **c)** 'd like

**10** It's a good idea to _____ more time with friends.
   **a)** save
   **b)** take
   **c)** spend

**11** She _____ sing at the party.
   **a)** doesn't going to
   **b)** isn't going to
   **c)** is going not to

**12** My favourite activity is _____ long walks.
   **a)** going in
   **b)** going for
   **c)** walking in

**13** I had dinner with _____.
   **a)** they
   **b)** us
   **c)** them

**14** I want to _____ smoking and _____ weight.
   **a)** stop, lose
   **b)** lose, get
   **c)** stop, save

**15 A:** Where did you buy this?
   **B:** I _____ it online.
   **a)** paid
   **b)** payed
   **c)** bought

**16 A:** Goodbye!
   **B:** See you _____ three weeks!
   **a)** at
   **b)** in
   **c)** after

**17** I like _____ up early, but I hate _____ breakfast alone.
   **a)** getting, having
   **b)** geting, having
   **c)** getting, haveing

**18** Oh _____, this is my station. I _____ we meet again!
   **a)** see, hope
   **b)** look, hope
   **c)** look, want

**19** _____ sing?
   **a)** Do you can
   **b)** Are you can
   **c)** Can you

**20** My daughter likes _____ photos.
   **a)** making
   **b)** taking
   **c)** doing

RESULT | /20

## LEAD IN Recording 1

1 one, two …
2 eight, nine …
3 five, six …
4 zero, one …
5 seven, eight …
6 three, four …

## LEAD IN Recording 2

phone
bus
number
chocolate
football
hotel

## LEAD IN Recording 3

**1**
A: We don't use verbs that way in our language.
B: I don't understand.
**2**
A: What's *autobus* in English?
B: It's *bus*.
**3**
A: Sorry, which page?
B: Seven.
**4**
A: I'm Marek.
B: Can you repeat that, please?
A: Marek.
**5**
A: What's *casa* in English?
B: Sorry, I don't know.
**6**
A: U-n-d-e-r-s-t-a-n-d.
B: Can you say it, please?
A: OK. Understand.

## UNIT 1 Recording 1

1 Spain
2 England, Ireland, Russia, Turkey, Poland, China
3 Japan, Brazil
4 Germany, Italy
5 Australia, South Africa

## UNIT 1 Recording 2

1 I'm an American student.
2 You're a New York taxi driver.
3 Are you an actor?
4 I'm an engineer from Madrid.
5 I'm a hotel waiter.
6 Are you a singer?

## UNIT 1 Recording 3

**1**
A: Excuse me? Am I in the Japanese class?
B: Yes, you are.
A: Are you the teacher?
B: No, I'm not. I'm a student.
A: Oh, sorry.
B: No problem. I'm Ed.
A: Hi, I'm Cathy. I'm a student, too.
B: Nice to meet you.
A: And you. Are you from Canada?
B: Yes, I am. And you, are you English?
A: No, I'm from Ireland.
B: Oh, here's Misaki, the teacher. She's from Japan.
**2**
A: Excuse me.
B: Yes?
A: Are you a nurse?
B: No, I'm a doctor.
A: Oh, sorry. I'm a nurse. My name's Anna. It's my first time here.
B: Oh, hello. I'm Lynn. Lynn Baker.
A: Nice to meet you, Doctor Baker. Are you from England?
B: Yes, I am. Look, here's a nurse. Jan, this is Anna.
C: Hi, Anna.
A: Hi.
C: Where are you from?
A: I'm from Poland.
C: Oh. *Dzien dobry!*
A: Are you from Poland, too?
C: No, I'm from Russia.

## UNIT 1 Recording 4

**1**
A: Good morning. I'm Sylvia White.
B: Ah, yes, Mrs White. You're in Room 9.
A: Is Mr Martin here?
B: Yes, he is. He's in Room 8.
**2**
A: Hi, Pat. Nice camera!
B: Thanks.
A: Is it a Panasonic?
B: No, it isn't. It's an Olympus.
**3**
A: Hi, Helena!
B: Oh, hello, Marcus. Marcus, this is Jackie, from Australia.
A: Hi, Jackie. Nice to meet you. Are you here on holiday?
C: No, I'm here on business.

## UNIT 1 Recording 5

1 SRNF
2 AKJE
3 GBIT
4 IIUWQ
5 VCYP
6 XZLD

## UNIT 1 Recording 6

**1**
A: My name's Alexandra Baecher.
B: How do you spell Baecher?
A: B-a-e-c-h-e-r.
**2**
A: Mr Mancini. What's your first name?
B: Giacomo.
A: That's J-a …
B: No, G-i-a-c-o-m-o.
A: G-i-a-c-o-m-o.
B: That's right.
**3**
A: Louise Walsh.
B: How do you spell Walsh?
A: W-a-l-s-h.
**4**
A: What's your name?
B: Vicky Watson.
A: Vicky Watson. How do you spell Vicky?
B: V-i-c-k-y.
**5**
A: Meilin Zhu.
B: Meilin … How do you spell Zhu?
A: Z-h-u.
B: Z-h-u.
**6**
A: Rufus Kean.
B: Rufus. How do you spell that?
A: R-u-f-u-s.
B: R-u-f-u-s. Rufus Kean. K-e-a-n?
A: That's right.

# AUDIO SCRIPTS

## UNIT 1 Recording 7

**1**
**A:** What's your email address?
**B:** It's yvesbedi373@yippee.com.
**A:** E-v. How do you spell your first name?
**B:** Not e-v. Y-v. Y as in, erm, yes. Y-v-e-s.

**2**
**A:** What's your email address?
**B:** It's johanna999@gomail.com.
**A:** Johanna999 … y-o-h …
**B:** No, j-o-h …
**A:** J?
**B:** J. J-o-h-a-n-n-a.
**A:** OK. Wait. A-n-n-a?
**B:** Yes. A-n-n-a.

**3**
**A:** And your email address?
**B:** Heidiho251@itmail.com.
**A:** H-e-i-d … Is it e as in England?
**B:** No, h-e-i-d-i. I as in it or in.
**A:** OK, heidiho251@itmail.com.
**B:** That's right.

**4**
**A:** My email address is jorgelopes@ toggle.com.
**B:** Just a minute. OK. G-o-r …
**A:** J not g. J-o-r …
**B:** J-o-r-g-e. Lopez?
**A:** Yes.
**B:** L-o-p-e … z as in zoo?
**A:** No, s as in, er, supermarket.
**B:** Lopes.
**A:** Yeah, jorgelopes@toggle.com.

## UNIT 2 Recording 1

I = Interviewer    B = Ben    C = Celeste

**1**
**I:** Ben, you're an actor.
**B:** Yes.
**I:** And you're from a family of actors.
**B:** Yes, my parents are actors.
**I:** And your brothers and sister?
**B:** Yes, my sister's a film actress and one of my brothers, Jack, is an actor. But my other brother, Dave, isn't in the acting business.
**I:** Oh, what's his job?
**B:** He's a teacher.
**I:** And is it a problem?
**B:** Is what a problem?
**I:** Well, your family are all in the same business. You're actors. You're from an acting family.
**B:** Well … OK, it is a problem sometimes.
**I:** For example?
**B:** Well, my parents and my brother are very good actors. And my sister – her films are very good and … well, it's new for me …
**I:** Ah, I understand. And …

**2**
**I:** Celeste, just a few questions.
**C:** Sure.
**I:** You're from a very big sports family. Your mother's a swimmer, your father's a footballer …
**C:** Yes.
**I:** And your sister's an international tennis player. In the top ten in the world.
**C:** That's right.
**I:** And you're a great sportswoman yourself, already at sixteen years old …
**C:** Seventeen.
**I:** Right, seventeen. You're the number two junior tennis player in the USA.
**C:** Yes.
**I:** So, is it a problem?
**C:** Is what a problem?
**I:** Well, your sister …
**C:** No, it's not a problem. But …

## UNIT 2 Recording 2

1 What's her job?
2 Where's she from?
3 Where's he from?
4 He's from Spain.
5 What's his surname?
6 Where's our bus?
7 Where's their room?

## UNIT 2 Recording 3

**A:** Let's have a break.
**B:** No, let's not stop. Let's work.
**A:** No, let's not work now.
**B:** Why not? What's the problem?
**A:** I'm tired!
**B:** Oh. Yes, I'm tired, too.
**A:** Let's stop.
**B:** Good idea!

## UNIT 2 Recording 4

**1a**
**A:** Let's eat.
**B:** Great.
**1b**
**A:** Let's eat.
**B:** Great.
**2a**
**A:** Let's go.
**B:** Good idea.
**2b**
**A:** Let's go.
**B:** Good idea.
**3a**
**A:** Let's stop.
**B:** OK.
**3b**
**A:** Let's stop.
**B:** OK.
**4a**
**A:** Let's have a drink.
**B:** Great idea.
**4b**
**A:** Let's have a drink.
**B:** Great idea.

## UNIT 2 Recording 5

**1**
**A:** Let's eat.
**B:** Great.
**2**
**A:** Let's go.
**B:** Good idea.
**3**
**A:** Let's stop.
**B:** OK.
**4**
**A:** Let's have a drink.
**B:** Great idea.

## REVIEW 1 Recording 1

1 brother
2 children
3 husband
4 actor
5 thirsty
6 daughter

## REVIEW 1   Recording 2

1 WAW
2 ICN
3 ESB
4 AMM
5 FCO
6 HEL
7 PEK
8 YOW
9 KUL
10 IAD
11 BER
12 DME

## REVIEW 1   Recording 3

1 WAW is Frederic Chopin Airport in Poland.
2 ICN is Incheon International Airport in Seoul, South Korea.
3 ESB is Esenboğa International Airport in Ankara, Turkey.
4 AMM is Queen Alia International Airport in Amman, Jordan.
5 FCO is Leonardo da Vinci-Fiucomo Airport near Rome, Italy.
6 HEL is Helsinki Vantaa Airport in Helsinki, Finland.
7 PEK is Beijing Capital International Airport in Beijing, China.
8 YOW is Ottawa International Airport in Ottawa, Canada.
9 KUL is Kuala Lumpur Airport near Kuala Lumpur, Malaysia.
10 IAD is Washington Dulles International Airport in Washington DC, the United States of America.
11 BER is Berlin Brandenburg Airport in Berlin, Germany.
12 DME is Domodedovo International Airport in Moscow, Russia.

## REVIEW 1   Recording 4

A: Oh, no! Five hours in the airport!
B: Yeah, five hours. Hey, I'm thirsty.
A: Yeah, me too. Let's have a drink.
B: Let's go to the café.
A: No, let's not go to the café. Let's go to the restaurant.
B: The restaurant? No, the café.
A: OK, OK. Let's go to the café.
B: Good idea!

## REVIEW 1   Recording 5

A: … and what's your name?
B: Erm, it's Adel.
A: Adel …
B: Adcl Gonda.
A: How do you spell that?
B: A-d-e-l, G-o-n-d-a.
A: A-d-a-l …
B: A-d-e-l …
A: A-d-e-l, G-o-n-t-a.
B: No, G-o-n-d-a.
A: OK. And what's your phone number?
B: It's four-five-seven-one-seven-six-two.
A: And what's your email address?
B: It's adel327@cmail.com.
A: A-d-e-l …
B: A-d-e-l-3-2-7at cmail …
A: S-m-a-i-l?
B: No, c-m-a-i-l.
A: Dot com?
B: Yes.

## UNIT 3   Recording 1

1 Is this your book here on the table?
2 What are these boxes here on my chair?
3 This is my friend, Domingo.
4 These are my parents, Steve and Beth.
5 Is that a number 43 bus over there?
6 Are those your books over there?
7 Who is that woman with Harry?
8 Who are those children?

## UNIT 3   Recording 2

1
A: Hello, can I ask you a question?
B: Yeah?
A: What's your favourite colour?
B: My favourite colour. Erm … I think it's red. Yes, red.
A: Why red?
B: Look, you can see. My T-shirt's red and my shoes.
A: Nice shoes.
B: Thanks. And of course my car is red.
A: Of course!

2
A: What's your favourite colour?
C: I don't know.
A: Is it blue, maybe? Your sweater's blue and your bag.
C: Yes, that's true, but no, I think my favourite colour is yellow.
A: Why?
C: Yellow's a happy colour. You know, the sun, the beach … it's a happy colour. Yes, yellow.

3
A: Excuse me. Have you got a minute?
D: Er … yes, OK.
A: Erm, what's your favourite colour?
D: Hmm. Well, these are my favourite trousers and jacket, and they're brown. So, brown, yes, brown. All my shoes are brown, too!

## UNIT 3   Recording 3

1
A: Good afternoon.
B: Hi. Erm … can we have two egg sandwiches, please?
A: On brown bread or white?
B: Er … brown, please. And two coffees – one espresso and one cappuccino.
A: That's two egg sandwiches on brown bread, an espresso and a cappuccino.
B: Thanks.

2
C: Excuse me.
A: Sorry, just a minute … Sorry, Madam. We're very busy.
C: No problem. Can I have a mineral water?
A: Still or sparkling?
C: Still, please.
A: Anything else?
C: Er, yes, can I have a cake?
A: A cake, right …
C: Er, no, make that two of those chocolate cakes.
A: Two. OK?
C: Yes. Two cakes, please.
A: And two cakes.

3
A: Can I help you?
D: Yes, can we have two colas and one tea … What's the problem, Kieron? What? No cola? OK, sorry. One cola, one water.
A: Mineral water?
D: Yes, sparkling mineral water.
A: So that's one cola, one sparkling mineral water and one tea.
D: That's right.
A: Anything else?
D: Yes. One cake, please.
A: OK. One cake.

# AUDIO SCRIPTS

**UNIT 4** Recording 1

1 What's your name?
2 Where do you live?
3 Why do you live in two cities?
4 Who do you live with?
5 What's your job?
6 Where do you work?

**UNIT 4** Recording 2

1 wants
2 does
3 teaches
4 listens
5 asks
6 stops
7 says
8 reads
9 knows
10 watches
11 writes
12 goes

**UNIT 4** Recording 3

I = Interviewer   A = Angela   M = Matt

**I:** Today's programme is about 'double lives' and we have in the studio a sister and brother, Angela …
**A:** Hi.
**I:** … and Matt.
**M:** Hello.
**I:** Angela and Matt are from Lancaster, in England. They're twins, they're thirty-six years old. And … well, let me ask you some questions. Angela, you and Matt have a taxi company, yes?
**A:** That's right. Twin Taxi Company.
**I:** So twin brother and sister, twin taxis – two taxis – good name for the company!
**A:** We don't have two taxis. We have one taxi.
**I:** Oh? So who drives?
**M:** Well, it's a twenty-four-hour taxi service. Well, actually twenty-two hours. I drive eleven hours and Angela drives eleven hours.
**I:** In the same taxi, day and night.
**A:** I drive in the morning and in the afternoon.
**M:** And I drive in the evening and at night.
**A:** And we love it. It's great!
**I:** Eleven hours a day. That's a lot of work.
**M:** Yes, well we both have children.
**A:** Yeah, and they always want something new – a new phone, new computer …
**M:** … new clothes, new shoes.
**I:** How many children do you have, Matt?
**M:** I have two children.
**I:** Twins?
**M:** No! A son and a daughter. He's three and she's four years old.
**I:** And you Angela?
**A:** One girl, Diana. She's seventeen.
**I:** OK. You both work a lot. When do you two see each other?
**A:** We have coffee together every morning at six.
**M:** Yeah, I stop work then …
**A:** … and I start work.
**I:** And what do you two usually talk about?
**M:** The usual, really – family, children, my wife …
**A:** … my husband, money.
**I:** The taxi?
**A/M:** Yes, the taxi!

**UNIT 4** Recording 4

1 Sunday
2 Tuesday
3 Thursday
4 Friday
5 Wednesday
6 Monday
7 Saturday

**UNIT 4** Recording 5

1
**A:** When are the English lessons?
**B:** We meet every Tuesday and Thursday at 7p.m.
2
**A:** See you on Friday!
**B:** OK. Let's meet in the evening for coffee.
3
**A:** Do you have work this week?
**B:** Yes, I work every day, and at the weekend, too.
4
**A:** Why are you so tired?
**B:** I work at night and go to university in the morning. I don't sleep!
5
**A:** Are you here tomorrow?
**B:** Yes, I'm here every morning, but not in the afternoon.

**UNIT 4** Recording 6

1 one o'clock
2 quarter past five
3 quarter to twelve
4 half past nine
5 quarter to seven
6 seven o'clock
7 quarter past four
8 half past two

**UNIT 4** Recording 7

1
**A:** What time's the football match?
**B:** The football match? At half past nine.
**A:** Sorry?
**B:** Half past nine.
**A:** Half past nine. OK, thanks.
2
**A:** Do you want to go to a party?
**B:** Maybe. What time does it start?
**A:** It starts at seven.
**B:** At seven? OK. Let's go!

**1**
**A:** What time is it now?
**B:** It's quarter to three.
**A:** So let's have a coffee.
**B:** Can I have a tea?
**2**
**A:** The film is at eight.
**B:** Oh, good, it's at ten.
**A:** Not ten, it's at eight!
**B:** Can you say that again?
**3**
**A:** Can I have water?
**B:** Sparkling or still?
**A:** I think I want sparkling. I feel very ill.
**4**
**A:** I'm tired and hungry.
**B:** So let's have a break.
**A:** Can I have a coffee?
**B:** Can I have a cake?

**UNIT 5**  Recording 1

1 **A:** Does Calvin come to class on time?
  **B:** Yes, he does.
2 **A:** Does he ask questions in class?
  **B:** Yes, he does.
3 **A:** Does he listen to the answers?
  **B:** No, he doesn't.
4 **A:** Does he speak English in class?
  **B:** No, he doesn't.
5 **A:** Does he write in the class blog?
  **B:** Yes, he does.
6 **A:** Does he read English books?
  **B:** No, he doesn't.
7 **A:** Does he watch films in English?
  **B:** Yes, he does.
8 **A:** Does he do his homework?
  **B:** No, he doesn't.

**UNIT 5**  Recording 2

I = Interviewer  G = George

**A:** So, George, you're a sumo wrestler.
**B:** That's right.
**A:** But you aren't Japanese?
**B:** No, I'm American. My parents are Japanese.
**A:** OK. So, my first question is … what do you eat?
**B:** Everyone asks that question! Do you mean, how am I so …
**A:** … big.
**B:** … fat?
**A:** OK, yeah. Do you eat a lot of food?
**B:** Yes, I do, but it's difficult.
**A:** So, what's a typical day?
**B:** Well, in a typical day, I get up at seven in the morning.
**A:** And do you have a big breakfast?
**B:** No, I don't. I never have breakfast.
**A:** Oh … I'm surprised … So what do you do in the morning?
**B:** I go to work. I do sport – sumo training.
**A:** And you aren't hungry? You do sport with no food …
**B:** Well, yes, I'm very hungry in the mornings … always.
**A:** When do you eat? Do you have lunch?
**B:** Yes, we have lunch together at twelve. A big lunch.
**A:** And do you eat junk food … pizza, hamburgers – things like that?
**B:** No, I never eat pizza or other junk food. I usually eat 'Chanko-nabe'.
**A:** 'Chanko-nabe'? What's that?
**B:** It's Japanese – it's with chicken, fish and vegetables.
**A:** Very healthy!
**B:** Yes, and I often have six litres of beer with lunch.
**A:** Really? Six litres?
**B:** And then, after lunch, I go to bed.
**A:** You go to bed!
**B:** Yes, I usually sleep about four hours in the afternoon.
**A:** And in the evening?
**B:** Sumo training … a big dinner of Chanko-nabe and beer, and then sleep. I usually go to bed at about ten.
**A:** Well, that's very interesting. Thank you, George. Now I'm er … hungry.
**B:** Let's have lunch!
**A:** Chanko-nabe?
**B:** Of course!

**UNIT 5**  Recording 3

1 gym
2 café, gift shop, restaurant
3 hairdresser's
4 swimming pool, guided tour
5 money exchange

**UNIT 5**  Recording 4

**A:** Excuse me?
**B:** Yes, can I help you?
**A:** When does the guided tour leave?
**B:** It leaves every hour from ten in the morning.
**A:** So at ten, eleven, twelve and so on?
**B:** Yes, at ten, eleven, twelve … then one, two, three, four and five. Oh, sorry, there isn't a guided tour at five today.
**A:** OK, thanks. Erm … what time does the ticket office open?
**B:** It opens at nine a.m., and ten a.m. on Sunday.
**A:** When does it close?
**B:** At five p.m. and at eight p.m. on Saturday. On Saturday we have an evening tour at eight.
**A:** How much does it cost?
**B:** It's twenty-five euros. And ten euros for children.
**A:** Right. Where does it leave from?
**B:** It leaves from the ticket office, but it stops here at the hotel, too.
**A:** Thank you very much.
**B:** You're welcome.

**UNIT 5**  Recording 5

**1**
**A:** Good morning.
**B:** Good morning. Can I help you?
**A:** Yes. What time is lunch?
**B:** It starts at twelve and finishes at two, but it's half past two now. I'm sorry.
**A:** That's a shame.
**2**
**C:** Excuse me?
**B:** Yes, can I help you?
**C:** Do you have a money exchange?
**B:** Yes, we do.
**C:** Great. What time does it open and close?
**B:** It opens at ten and closes at four.
**C:** Right. Thank you.
**3**
**B:** Good afternoon. Can I help you?
**D:** Yes, do you have a map of the city?
**B:** Yes, here you are.
**D:** Great, thanks.
**B:** You're welcome.

# AUDIO SCRIPTS

## UNIT 6   Recording 1

1 café
2 internet café
3 hotel
4 payphone
5 newsagent's
6 cash machine
7 restaurant
8 pharmacy

## UNIT 6   Recording 2

**1**
A: North Street, please.
B: Do you have any bags?
A: Yes, these, but they're OK here.
B: North Street?
A: Yes, the Garden Hotel.
B: Right, I know it. Where are you from?
C: We're from New Zealand, Auckland.
B: Ah … and is this your first time in Belfast?
C: Yes, and it's our first time in Ireland.
A: We're on holiday here, for two weeks.
B: Ah, well, it's a good time to visit because …

**2**
A: Tea or coffee, sir?
B: Er … coffee, please.
A: With milk?
B: Yes, and can I have sugar, please? Er, what time is it in Moscow now?
A: It's … er, quarter to three.
B: And do you know … about the weather?
A: Yes, it's hot. It's thirty degrees.
B: That's hot. Thanks.
A: Enjoy your drink.

**3**
A: Do you go to the city centre?
B: Where do you want to go?
A: To the Summer Café. In Old Street.
B: Yes, we go there.
A: OK, one adult and two children, please.
B: That's two fifty.
A: I don't know the town. Can you tell us when we get there?
B: Yes, no problem. It's … er … five stops from here.

## UNIT 6   Recording 3

1 single ticket
2 ticket office
3 return ticket
4 passenger
5 monthly pass
6 gate

## UNIT 6   Recording 4

A: A ticket to Canberra, please.
B: Single or return?
A: Return, please.
B: For today?
A: Sorry, no, for tomorrow.
B: When do you want to go?
A: In the afternoon.
B: And when do you want to come back?
A: On Friday, in the morning.
B: OK, that's eighty-three dollars.
A: What time's the bus?
B: There's one at quarter to nine.
A: When does it arrive in Canberra?
B: At quarter to eleven.
A: Thanks a lot.

## UNIT 6   Recording 5

**1**
A: It's bus number thirty-nine.
B: Sorry? Twenty-nine?
A: No, thirty-nine.
**2**
A: That's forty-nine euros.
B: Sorry? Forty-five?
A: No, forty-nine.
**3**
A: The plane leaves from gate fifty-eight.
B: Sorry? Gate eighty-eight?
A: No, gate fifty-eight.
**4**
A: The bus leaves at quarter past five.
B: Sorry? Quarter to five?
A: No, quarter past five.
**5**
A: I'm fifty-four years old.
B: Sorry, sixty-four?
A: No, fifty-four.

## REVIEW 3   Recording 1

**1**
A: And here's your room key. Anything else?
B: Yes. Is there a café in the hotel?
A: No, there isn't. There's a restaurant.
B: And is breakfast in the restaurant?
A: Yes. Breakfast is in the restaurant from half past six.
B: Great. When does the restaurant open for dinner?
A: Breakfast is from half past six to eleven, lunch from eleven to three.
B: And dinner?
A: From five to ten.
B: Five to ten. OK, thank you.

**2**
A: Can I help you?
B: Yes, I'm a tourist here. I'm here for three days. What is there to do?
A: Well, there's a very good guided tour of the old town.
B: Is it a walking tour?
A: No, it's a bus tour. The old town's very big.
B: What time does it leave?
A: There's a tour at quarter past ten. Oh wait, it's half past ten now, sorry. So, the next tour is at half past one in the afternoon. And there's one at quarter to four.
B: Great. How much does it cost?
A: Seventeen euros.
B: Seventeen euros. OK.
A: OK, so … Do you like the theatre?
B: Yes, I do. Very much.
A: Well, we have summer theatre in the park now.
B: Lovely. When is it?
A: Hmm … Today's Monday, so there's no theatre.
B: Oh?
A: Tonight there's a concert in the park. At eight o'clock.
B: Wonderful. How much is it?
A: It's free.
B: Great. Free. And the theatre? When is that?
A: Tomorrow at half past seven.
B: How much is it?
A: Twenty-five euros.
B: OK, thanks.

**3**
A: Excuse me?
B: Yes, can I help you?
A: When is the next train to Brighton?
B: To Brighton? Let's see … it's a quarter to two now. There's a train at two, but it's a slow train.
A: That's OK. Can I have two tickets, please?
B: Single or return?
A: Return, please.
B: When do you want to come back?
A: We don't know.
B: OK. That's thirty-six pounds, please.
A: Thirty-six pounds?
B: Yes, eighteen pounds for one return.
A: OK.
B: Put your card in …

## REVIEW 3 Recording 2

**1**
A: And here's your room key. Anything else?
B: Yes. Is there a café in the hotel?
A: No, there isn't. There's a restaurant.

**2**
A: Breakfast is in the restaurant from half past six.
B: Great. When does the restaurant open for dinner?
A: From five to ten.

**3**
A: No, it's a bus tour. The old town's very big.
B: What time does it leave?
A: There's a tour at quarter past ten.

**4**
A: And there's one at quarter to four.
B: Great. How much does it cost?
A: Seventeen euros.

**5**
A: When is the next train to Brighton?
B: To Brighton? Let's see … it's a quarter to two now. There's a train at two, but it's a slow train.

**6**
A: Return, please.
B: When do you want to come back?
A: We don't know.

## UNIT 7 Recording 1

1 New Year's Day is the first of January.
2 Valentine's Day is the fourteenth of February.
3 The first of May is May Day.
4 Independence Day in the USA is the fourth of July.
5 International Women's Day is the eighth of March.
6 The eleventh of August is Son and Daughter's Day.
7 The twenty-fifth of December is Christmas Day.
8 The tenth of June is Children's Day.
9 The second of April is Children's Book Day.
10 Halloween is the thirty-first of October.

## UNIT 7 Recording 2

1 travel
2 try
3 move
4 play
5 arrive
6 start
7 talk
8 walk
9 wait
10 stop

## UNIT 7 Recording 3

1 Emperor penguins are very big, but every winter they go on a very long walk. Every year, the penguins walk between fifty and a hundred and twenty kilometres in the snow to find food in the sea.
2 A black and white cat named Tom was lost in a British Airways plane for two months. In these two months he travelled about eight hundred thousand kilometres and visited a lot of different countries.
3 Another amazing cat named Tom was a great traveller. He was from the USA and his family moved home from Florida to California, but Tom wasn't with them. He was left in Florida. Tom walked four thousand kilometres to find his family. He arrived at the new house in California after two years.
4 Everybody knows that milk comes from cows, not from the supermarket. The average cow gives two hundred thousand glasses of milk in its lifetime – and its lifetime is sometimes twenty-five years long!
5 Many parrots talk, but they don't know a lot of words – maybe ten or twenty. In 2004, in a test, N'kisi, an African grey parrot, used 950 words.

## UNIT 7 Recording 4

1 lived
2 closed
3 opened
4 listened
5 looked
6 studied
7 emailed
8 texted
9 stopped
10 answered

## UNIT 7 Recording 5

1 worked
2 wanted
3 asked
4 played
5 repeated
6 watched

## UNIT 7 Recording 6

**1**
A: How's your food?
B: mm-MM-m.
**2**
A: How's your food?
B: MM-mm-m.
**3**
A: How's your food?
B: MM.
**4**
A: How's your food?
B: MM-MM.
**5**
A: How's your food?
B: MM-mm.

## UNIT 7 Recording 7

1 mm-MM-m, delicious
2 MM-mm-m, terrible
3 MM, great
4 MM-MM, all right
5 MM-mm, awful

## UNIT 8 Recording 1

J = Jocelyn   A = Andreas

J: I met Clare last year in an Italian class. I wanted to learn Italian because I love Italy and I wanted to go to Italy on holiday. Anyway, Clare sat next to me in class. At first, I didn't like her, because she was good at Italian and I wasn't very good. But every day we went home on the same bus and we talked and became friends.
Then one day Clare phoned me and said, 'Hey, let's go to India together!' I was very surprised. I said, 'You mean Italy, not India.' She said 'No, India,' because she loved Indian food. I love it, too. We went to India together last summer and we had a fantastic time. We're great friends now.

A: I met my best friend Raji on the internet. It was in 2007, after I finished university. My first job was in Canberra. So I moved home, from Sydney to Canberra. All my friends were in Sydney and I didn't know anyone in Canberra.
I was bored in the evenings and I had a lot of free time. So I went on the internet a lot. And there was a blog, called Vindaloo, about Indian food. I love Indian food. And on the blog I talked to a guy called Raji. He knew a lot about Indian cooking. So I emailed him and I got an email back. He lived in Canberra, too. So we met, and we were instant best friends.

## UNIT 8   Recording 2

**1**
**A:** Excuse me. Where's the underground?
**B:** It's near the cash machine.
**A:** Opposite the trains?
**B:** Yes, that's right.

**2**
**A:** Excuse me. Where are the men's toilets?
**B:** They're on the right of the cash machine.

**3**
**A:** Excuse me. Where are the women's toilets?
**B:** They're on the right of the men's toilets.
**A:** On the right of the men's toilets?
**B:** And opposite the café.
**A:** OK, thanks.

**4**
**A:** Excuse me. Where are the taxis?
**B:** They're on the left of the buses.
**A:** So between the buses and the café?
**B:** Yes.
**A:** Thank you.

## UNIT 8   Recording 3

**1**
**A:** Oh, you're a teacher. And what's your husband's job?
**B:** What's that?
**A:** You know – doctor, teacher, secretary.
**B:** Oh! He's a pilot.

**2**
**A:** What fruit do they have in the supermarket today?
**B:** I don't understand.
**A:** Like, do they have apples, bananas, oranges?
**B:** Oh, OK. They have apples and oranges.

**3**
**A:** Do you know another adjective for 'good'?
**B:** Another what?
**A:** For example, good, bad, hot, cold, happy …
**B:** Oh, I understand. I know another word for 'very good'. Fantastic!

## REVIEW 4   Recording 1

1 liked
2 started
3 spoke
4 knew
5 cried
6 looked
7 wanted
8 talked
9 became
10 said
11 took
12 thought
13 stopped
14 listened
15 studied
16 met

## REVIEW 4   Recording 2

**1**
**A:** Is there a good restaurant near here?
**B:** There's a good Chinese restaurant over there.
**A:** Where?
**B:** On the left of the bank.
**A:** I see it. Is the food good?
**B:** Well, I think it's delicious.

**2**
**A:** Do you know the Chinese restaurant near here?
**C:** Yes.
**A:** Is it good?
**C:** It's all right, but I like Italian food. There's a great Italian restaurant opposite the school.
**A:** Where?
**C:** Behind the bus over there. Next to the newsagent's.
**A:** Oh, right. Yes. How's the food there?
**C:** We ate there last night. It was fantastic.

## UNIT 9   Recording 1

**Speaker 1**
I'm not a dancer, so I wasn't very good. I liked the music, you know, and I went with Cheryl – she's a great dancer. We laughed a lot. It was fantastic. I'm happy that we went, it was a great gift.

**Speaker 2**
It's just so fast. I mean, I usually drive fast, 120 kilometres an hour on the motorway, but this was different. You don't have time to think. I was really scared. I didn't like it. I thought it was too dangerous.

**Speaker 3**
Amazing, really. Everything was so small from up there, so far away. I felt relaxed, very relaxed. We took hundreds of pictures. The countryside was beautiful.

**Speaker 4**
We were a small group – five of us. We went out to this place near the sea. A very quiet, beautiful place. We sat and waited. And waited. We didn't speak. Our guide said, 'Just wait.' And then two or three birds were there, but nothing 'amazing'. The guide said it was a bad day for it, sometimes they don't come. So it wasn't very good, really. I was angry because I know it was expensive.

## UNIT 9   Recording 2

**1**
**A:** What would you like?
**B:** I'd like a cheese sandwich.
**A:** Would you like white bread or brown?
**B:** Brown, please.

**2**
**A:** Can I help you?
**B:** Yes, I'd like that sweater, please.
**A:** This one?
**B:** No. I'd like that brown one, please.

**3**
**A:** Come in. Sit down.
**B:** Nice flat!
**A:** Thanks. Would you like a drink?
**B:** Yes, I'd love an apple juice or something.

## UNIT 9   Recording 3

1 How was the weather yesterday?
2 How do you spell *beautiful*?
3 What would you like for dinner?
4 Where is your best friend now?

## UNIT 9 Recording 4

**1**
**A:** How was the weather yesterday?
**B:** Let me think. Um, it was sunny and cold …

**2**
**A:** How do you spell *beautiful*?
**B:** Er … b-e-a-u-t-i-f-u-l.

**3**
**A:** What would you like for dinner?
**B:** Well … Oh, I don't know.

**4**
**A:** Where is your best friend now?
**B:** Let me see … she's in California, I think.

## UNIT 10 Recording 1

**Speaker 1**
I started the job on Friday, and the first day was OK. But then on Saturday, a lot of people came into the shop and there were only two of us. People asked me questions and I didn't know the answers. I know about computers, but I don't know the shop or the prices of things. So some customers became angry. It was very difficult. My boss wasn't happy with me.

**Speaker 2**
I studied a long time for this job. I know the city and all the tourist places. I speak three languages: English, German and Japanese. Then on my first day, they gave me a group of Japanese tourists. I said 'Hello' in Japanese, and they said nothing. Nothing! I thought OK, let's do the tour. So we walked around the old town, I talked in Japanese about everything – my Japanese is really good. They all looked unhappy, but they didn't say anything. Then finally at the end one man said to me in English, 'We're not Japanese, we're Korean. We didn't understand you.' What a terrible mistake! I felt very bad.

**Speaker 3**
People think it's an easy job, but it isn't. I started one month ago and things were OK, but then a woman came in and asked for a simple hair cut. 'Just a little cut,' she said, 'and a shampoo.' I cut her hair and washed it, and then when she looked in the mirror, she screamed 'Arrrggh! It's too short!' Then I made a big mistake. I laughed. I didn't see a problem – her hair was good. Then my boss came out and he said, 'Go!' so I left. I thought I lost the job. An hour later he phoned me. He wasn't angry, he just said, 'Come back, but next time, don't laugh! OK?'

## UNIT 10 Recording 2

**1** He can't remember names, but he can remember numbers.
**2** She can swim, but she can't ride a bike.
**3** He can't drive a car, but he can ride a horse.
**4** She can throw, but she can't catch.
**5** He can play the guitar, but he can't sing.
**6** She can't cook, but she can make coffee.

## UNIT 10 Recording 3

**1**
**A:** What do you think of the food?
**B:** I think it's really good. It's a nice restaurant.
**A:** Let's have a coffee.
**B:** No, thanks. It's very late.
**A:** Oh … is that the time? My train is at eleven o'clock.
**B:** Yes. And I have a meeting tomorrow at eight o'clock.
**A:** Oh! That's early!

**2**
**A:** Hi, how are you?
**B:** I'm fine, thanks. I'm Katie.
**A:** I'm Sam. This is a great party.
**B:** Yes, it's really good. So are you from around here?
**A:** No, I'm from Sydney in Australia. Er … I'm sorry, I can see an old friend over there.
**B:** Oh. Well … nice to talk to you.
**A:** You too. I hope we meet again.
**B:** Yes. Maybe.

## UNIT 10 Recording 4

**1**
**A:** I hope you're at the party on Friday.
**B:** I hope so, too.

**2**
**A:** This is a nice place.
**B:** Yes, it's really good.

**3**
**A:** I hope you like the film.
**B:** I hope so, too.

**4**
**A:** This is my email address.
**B:** Here's mine.

**5**
**A:** I like this restaurant!
**B:** Yes, it's really good.

**6**
**A:** Here's my card.
**B:** Here's mine.

**7**
**A:** I hope we meet again.
**B:** I hope so, too.

**8**
**A:** Very nice to meet you.
**B:** You too.

## REVIEW 5 Recording 1

**1**
**A:** Good morning. Would you like a drink?
**B:** It's very hot. Um … I can't think.
**A:** Well, would you like a cup of tea?
**B:** Nice idea. Can I have three?

**2**
**A:** Is that the time? My train's at three.
**B:** Here's my card. James Bond – that's me.
**A:** Goodbye. I hope we meet again.
**B:** Let's meet tonight at half past ten.

**3**
**A:** This is my friend from work, Marty.
**B:** Nice to meet you. How's the party?
**C:** The music's bad, I hate this place, but nice to see a friendly face.

**4**
**A:** Sorry, I can see an old friend over there, the woman near the office chair.
**B:** That's not your friend! That's my wife, Flo.
**A:** Well, nice to meet you. Time to go!

**Pearson Education Limited**
Edinburgh Gate
Harlow
Essex CM20 2JE
England
and Associated Companies throughout the world.

www.pearsonelt.com

© Pearson Education Limited 2016

The right of Frances Eales, Steve Oakes and Stephanie Dimond-Bayir to be identified
as authors of this Work has been asserted by them in accordance with the Copyright,
Designs and Patents Act 1988.

First published 2016
Twelfth impression 2020
ISBN: 978-1-292-11448-4

Set in Aptifer sans 10/12 pt
Printed in Italy by L.E.G.O. Spa

**Illustration acknowledgements**
Illustrated by Eric@kja-artists

**Photo acknowledgements**
The publisher would like to thank the following for their kind permission to reproduce
their photographs:

(Key: b-bottom; c-centre; l-left; r-right; t-top)

**123RF.com:** 24tr, 33r, 39tr, 39bc (l), 39bc (r), 59br, 66, Selivanov Iurii 39tc (r);
**Alamy Images:** Blend Images 35, Hayden Richard Verry 7r, imagebroker 9tl; **Corbis:**
H. Armstrong Roberts / Classicstock 55, Reuters 48; **Fotolia.com:** al62 23tl,
ArenaCreative 7c, BillionPhotos.com 11, Deyan Georgiev 39br, Victoria Lipov 24tl,
Monkey Business 33l, 61, 62, Photocreo Bednarek 9br, ViewApart 59tr, Ints Vikmanis
56; **Getty Images:** Andersen Ross 63, Hill Street Studios 32b, Ljiljana Pavkov 24b;
**Pearson Education Ltd:** Jules Selmes 38tl; **PhotoDisc:** John A. Rizzo 34tl, Photolink
19tl; **Shutterstock.com:** Africa Studio 34c, Andresr 16, 29, Andresr. 7l, Andrjuss 34cr,
Alexey Boldin 58, Dr.OGA 19tr, Elena Elisseeva 34bl, Ron Ellis 38, Szasz-Fabian Jozsef
23tr, Gemenacom 59bl, grafvision 34t, Patricia Hofmeester 9bl, Byelikova Oksana
9tr, Dan Peretz 34cl, Elena Schweitzer. 19br, Sergio33 23bl, Skymax 59tl, Ljupco
Smokovski. 39tc (l), stefanel 19bl, v.s.anandhakrishna 23br, Vacclav. 53, VadiCo 34br,
Dani Vincek 34tr, Krivosheev Vitaly 39bl

All other images © Pearson Education

Every effort has been made to trace the copyright holders and we apologise
in advance for any unintentional omissions. We would be pleased to insert the
appropriate acknowledgement in any subsequent edition of this publication.